THINKING ABOUT TRANSPORT

LESSONS FROM LANGDONS

A Langdons truck through mountain scenery.

THINKING ABOUT TRANSPORT

LESSONS FROM LANGDONS

R.W. HOLDER

PHILLIMORE

2008

Published by
PHILLIMORE & CO. LTD
Chichester, West Sussex, England
www.phillimore.co.uk
www.thehistorypress.co.uk

ISBN 978-1-86077-537-6

Printed and bound in Great Britain

Contents

LIST OF ILLUSTRATIONS

Frontispiece: A Langdons truck through mountain scenery.

PROLOGUE

Lady Day, 25 March, seemed an auspicious date on which to hold an auction. That brisk morning in 1997 Michael Donoghue, Managing Director of the Somerset-based haulier Langdons, watched while eight of the firm's articulated prime movers (or tractors) and 28 of its curtain-sided trailers were sold at auction. For his competitors the gathering was something of a festive occasion, although it elicited a certain amount of sympathy. Eleven years earlier Michael had led a management buy-out of Langdons and since then had overseen the transformation of an unprofitable jobbing transport business which had operated an assortment of hired and obsolete equipment, heavily dependent on owner-drivers. With its new vehicles and smart livery, coupled with a reputation for reliability, Langdons had been picking up too many major contracts for the ease of mind of its competitors. In particular it had built up its relationship with the locally based Taunton Cider Company to the extent that it was their only haulier, delivering some forty loads a day. The word in the trade was that Langdons had been about to take over Taunton Cider's fleet of vehicles and distribution warehouse, which would have made its exclusive position even more impregnable.

Langdons had become too much of a threat for there not to be a certain amount of schadenfreude among some of those attending the auction, but there was also much sympathy for Michael, who was well known in the industry and well liked. The bidding was brisk because the equipment was relatively new and in good order. When the hammer descended on the last lot, the sale had generated £284,000 plus Value Added Tax. It was now time for the bidders to join Michael and me in a nearby pub, the *Cross Keys*, where we received commiseration from our competitors and allowed ourselves to enjoy their hospitality.

Eleven years before the sale, Langdons had owned only two roadworthy prime movers and a few obsolescent trailers. Eleven years after the sale it owned 200 prime movers, was operating six depots, had a turnover of £50 million a year and enjoyed one of the highest profit margins in the industry. This is the story of how it happened.

Chapter One

HOW IT STARTED

*T*aunton Cider and Langdons, which was published in 2000, described how two West Somerset businesses had grown from the most modest of beginnings to become major employers in the region. The book also examined the development of regional communications and the technical advances in transportation which had occurred in the century or more during which both businesses operated. After a management buy-out in 1986, Langdons had worked more and more closely with Taunton Cider, each company becoming increasingly dependent on the other. That relationship, and its rupture, is germane to what happened after the sale of much of Langdons' equipment in 1997. This account, however, is not concerned with the unhappy fate of those who worked for the cider company, nor need we go into great detail about the origins of Langdons. Those wanting to read the full account must consult the earlier book because here you will find only the salient outline.

Langdons can claim to have started in business in June 1897, when a 15-year-old farmer's daughter called Bessie Hill walked the two miles from Ridge Farm into the market town of Wiveliscombe carrying a gross of eggs to sell to a local grocer. With the hot weather the grocer had a surfeit of eggs, and he paid Bessie the niggardly price of five shillings for the lot, or fivepence a dozen. Farmer Hill had an arrangement with a Bristol provision merchant called Jesse Watkins, to whom he regularly dispatched butter by train, getting a better net price than he would selling it in Wiveliscombe. Returning to the farm that day, Bessie sat down and wrote to Mr Watkins, offering to supply him with eggs as her father did with butter. In reply, he offered to take all her eggs at ninepence a dozen so long as they were individually packed in newspaper. From then on the parliamentary train in the evening from Wiveliscombe to Taunton and then on to Bristol carried her eggs as well as Mr Hill's butter.

Before long, Bessie's own hens were unable to satisfy the demand from Mr Watkins and she started collecting from surrounding farms, charging a penny an egg as a handling fee. She used her pony and a trap for the collection of eggs and delivery to Wiveliscombe station, relying on the efficient railway goods service to maintain her daily commitment to Bristol. Years later, after

Bessie Hill had become Bessie Langdon by marrying a saddler, she entered into another contract to supply eggs to London, again using the railway for transportation.

When hens stop laying they are still saleable for eating. Traders calling on the farms paid poor prices for these birds, and young Bessie Hill started buying them, again using her contact in Bristol as an outlet for the meat. As with the eggs, demand soon exceeded supply and Bessie moved into chicken farming, eventually buying up other firms of chicken producers and employing over 200 people in Wivesliscombe, Milverton and Taunton. As the business developed, three vans replaced the horse and trap for local collection, and by the 1920s most of her produce, which now included rabbit meat as well and chickens and eggs, was going to London rather than to Bristol.

Until the 1930s the railway network, with its entrepôt facilities, rapid service and ability to deliver to the eventual customer, dominated the British transportation and distribution market. Local carriers for the most part only ferried goods to or from the railway. The cost of freight nationally was set by the railway. The canals still carried some traffic in minerals and timber, but long-distance road transport was no threat to rail. The single-carriageway roads threaded their tortuous way through the centre of every town and village. Lorries carried limited loads and were mechanically unreliable, liable to break down far from the skimpy repair facilities. The average speed achieved on a long journey by a motor truck was much slower than a comparable journey by rail, which was an important factor when perishable goods such as meat were being delivered in vehicles without temperature control. There were no speed limits on the roads before 1936 but goods vehicles, even the petrol-driven lorries which were replacing those powered by steam, were incapable of speeding.

The event which started the transformation of Bessie Langdon's business into a transport company took place between 1 and 12 May 1926, when Britain experienced its General Strike. As many as 849 trains ran on the first day of the strike, and by the start of the second week the figure had grown to five thousand. But the damage had been done, even though London's food supplies had been protected when 100 lorries were escorted by armoured cars into Hyde Park. Having seen the necessity for road transport, producers and manufacturers throughout the country decided there was too great a risk ever again to rely solely on the railway network for their distribution. And without distribution, producers and manufacturers have no business.

During the strike the Wiveliscombe-based brewers Arnold and Hancock used a lorry to collect raw material from Bristol. They offered to carry Mrs Langdon's eggs there on the outward leg if she would provide a man to ride shotgun as a protection against violence from the strikers. There was no violence and no eggs were thrown or broken. To protect her business from further risk of disruption, in 1927 she bought a Chevrolet three-ton lorry which her son Bill, with a co-driver, used for deliveries to London, either to supplement or supplant the railway. Her fleet was still only three local delivery vans and one lorry, but she was now peripherally in the transport business.

Mrs Langdon never attended a business school, but her career illustrates fundamental rules which are as valid now as they were then.

- Your optimum market is not necessarily the nearest.
- Use a reliable third party to manage distribution away from your home base if you cannot justify setting up a subsidiary.
- Ensure that you do not place yourself at the mercy of a single third party for any essential part of the business.
- Expand your business by moving into related trades.
- Always honour your commitments.
- Without efficient and reliable distribution, you have no business.

Chapter 2

THE MOVE FROM POULTRY INTO TRANSPORT

Most of us reach major decisions after due consideration of reasons and motives which we are not philosophical enough to analyse. Bessie Langdon may have been considering buying a lorry of her own for deliveries to London before the General Strike, but that event, and the possibility that it might happen again, would have concentrated her thoughts. Apart from that, she had the experience of operating three motor vans for local work and her elder son, Bill, was a mechanic who was more interested in engineering than in chicken farming. In the summer of 1927 she had sent several consignments of rabbit meat to London by rail, only to have them rejected by customers because they had become unfit for eating due to the delays in handling. The tipping point arrived when a consignment of chickens for a City banquet was allowed to go off through a mistake by railway staff, resulting in a lot of inedible carcasses, disappointed diners and, for Bessie, a lost customer. To compound matters, the railway declined to accept responsibility for its error.

Bill drove and maintained the Chevrolet, using it to make direct deliveries to London and weekly journeys to Southampton to supply the great ocean liners. In those days there were no limitations on the hours drivers might work or the rests they should take. To correspond with the rail timetable with which London customers had become familiar, Bill and his co-driver would leave Wiveliscombe at 6 p.m. and be back by 9 o'clock the next morning. The lorry was then used by another driver during the day for local collection before setting off with a distant delivery the next evening.

The driver of a delivery lorry in the 1930s required both skill and muscle. If the vehicle broke down he would be expected to carry out any minor repair himself. Tyres punctured easily. There were no pallets or fork-lift trucks. The driver and his mate had to load and unload everything by hand, and on one occasion to load, unload and reload. (On the eve of the maiden voyage of the liner the *Queen Mary* in 1935, Bill took supplies of eggs to Southampton docks and unloaded them while dockers stood by and watched. He was then told to put them back on the lorry as unloading was dockers' work.)

In 1930 Bill started using the lorry for bringing loads of feed back from Bristol for local farmers. This can be seen as another step towards becoming a haulage company. Return loading is the secret of success for a common carrier, which is why firms who use their own vehicles for delivery are usually wasting money unless they have internal traffic in both directions.

When the First World War started in 1914, the authorities had requisitioned Bessie's horse. In 1939 the Chevrolet suffered the same fate. Bill and his younger brother, Philip, joined the forces, leaving their mother and sister to run the egg and poultry business. In passing, we may wonder what state of preparedness for war the nation found itself in to have needed the use of a 12-year-old lorry.

After the war Bill and Philip returned to work for their mother in the egg and poultry business. The Labour government had nationalised the road haulage industry and it was not until 1955 that private operators were allowed to operate as general hauliers. The government had controlled its monopoly through the licensing of individual vehicles. A 'C' licence, which was not difficult to obtain, allowed a trader to carry his own goods in his own vehicle. A 'B' licence, more difficult, allowed a trader to haul his own goods and those of specified third parties but limited to certain types of cargo or geographical locations. The 'A' licences, allowing carriage for anyone without restriction, were initially held by the nationalised body, operating under the sometimes misleading name of British Road Services (BRS).

The initial break-up of the monopoly was effected by allowing an 'A' licence to be transferred to a new operator with the vehicle to which the licence was attached, but to get the licence you had to buy the vehicle. The BRS managers fiercely resisted any applications by private traders for new 'A' licences, and for a while the only way to get decent equipment was to buy an old lorry with an 'A' licence, scrap the lorry, and transfer the licence to a new vehicle.

In 1956 Bessie Langdon retired. She handed control of her business to her two sons and went to see her daughter who lived in Australia. Bill wasted no time in engaging an experienced haulier called Sidney Pulsford to help him re-enter the transport business in Wiveliscombe, delivering the firm's produce to London and picking up feedstuffs from Avonmouth on the return trip. Within two years his fleet had grown to 17 vehicles and the company, operating as Tone Vale Transport Ltd, was engaged in warehousing as well as general haulage. In addition to Mr Pulsford, Bill recruited a transport operator called Kenneth Thorne as a manager.

In 1960 Philip obtained control of three lorries with 'A' licences operating from Taunton in the temperature-controlled haulage of meat, and established a company called Taunton Meat Haulage Ltd. The deal had been set up and fronted by Tom Hewett, who stayed on as manager under Philip. Like Tone Vale Transport, the business grew rapidly and included a substantial Irish trade. At that time meat carcasses were carried on hooks inside specialist lorries, rather than being jointed at the abattoir and repacked, as most of them are today. Although there was a certain amount of reciprocal business between the two Langdon haulage companies, each was run independently of the other.

Bill and Philip Langdon were dissimilar in character. Bill was a mechanic who had spent years on the road. He was well liked by his drivers because they

1 *A Tone Vale Transport flat-bed in the 1970s.*

knew he understood the world in which they operated and had done the job himself. Philip was an old-style proprietor of a private business, where the boss laid down the rules and employees obeyed them. Where Bill was conciliatory, Philip tended to be confrontational. When their mother was alive and in control of the business, they both had to toe the line. Unhappily, she died of measles in 1957, leaving the business to her sons but no longer there to keep the peace between them. Logic and economy suggested that the two businesses should be amalgamated, and not running two traffic offices, two maintenance garages, two sets of accounts, and so on, but in view of the brothers' different characters, it was sensible to keep them separate. They did, however, agree that if either of them died the other should take over the entire operation. In 1962, with larger national firms beginning to control the poultry and egg market, they also agreed to sell that business, keeping only the transport and storage.

On 5 April 1967 Bill Langdon died. Philip thereupon paid his sister-in-law £15,000 and took control of Tone Vale Transport as well as Taunton Meat Haulage. He voted Bill's son, Peter, who had been a director of the companies,

2 *A Taunton Meat Haulage refrigerated rig in 1970.*

off the boards. He also dispensed with Mr Pulsford, who had gone blind. Under Philip as the sole proprietor, Ken Thorne managed the ambient and Tom Hewett the temperature-controlled businesses. It might have seemed logical at that stage to amalgamate the two operations under one manager with a single traffic office, but that was not Philip Langdon's style. Instead he bought 'A' licences for the Taunton temperature-controlled operation from a Wellington company and a seven-vehicle ambient operation in Barnstaple, which he closed down, transferring the licences to Wiveliscombe.

The two businesses traded profitably until Philip decided to cut the Taunton Meat Haulage drivers' meal allowance by two shillings a day. The drivers went on strike and Philip dismissed them. The consequent disruption in service led to him losing his biggest customer, the Somerset meat company Lloyd Maunder. Taunton Meat Haulage had other work, especially the delivery of New Zealand lamb and butter from Avonmouth docks, but it is uneconomical to have your outward traffic originating some 50 miles from your home base, which is the distance between Taunton and Avonmouth, the journey involving the notoriously slow and congested A38 road. What with the loss of his drivers and of his best customer, and a disastrous warehouse fire in Wiveliscombe, Philip Langdon had had enough of trading on his own. In 1974 he sold the businesses to a conglomerate called Price and Pierce, staying on as Executive Chairman.

Philip had been obliged to replace his drivers with men who owned their own tractors, paid the company a percentage of their revenue and worked only for him. The owner-driver concept originated in the ready-mixed cement business and, for someone who had been at odds with the Transport and General Workers Union, it was about the only way he could stay in business. We will take a closer look at the advantages and disadvantages of owner-drivers in the transport industry, but with the Langdon companies becoming the subsidiary of a publicly quoted company, we can glean what lessons we have learned from the events so far.

- A business only exists so long as it has customers. If a good customer complains, pay attention.
- Never assume that competitors will let you retain a unique selling proposition.
- Every employee is important or should not be on the payroll. Employees need respect and consideration as much as customers.
- Being sole proprietor or Chairman of a business is a difficult and lonely job. You need somebody in the team who can monitor your actions and act as a sounding board.
- Divide and rule is a bad management philosophy.
- Don't duplicate overhead operations.
- Have your outward loads originating as near your base as possible.

Chapter 3

LIFE IN A CONGLOMERATE AND NEW MANAGEMENT

Before selling his transport companies to Price and Pierce, Philip Langdon had been in negotiation with a company in Southampton. No details of those discussions exist but it is probable that the other party was a haulage firm called Solent Shipping and Navigation Ltd (Solent), managed by Jack Fossett. The relationship between Philip Langdon and Solent did not end when he sold to someone else, although its precise nature remains shrouded in mystery. Ken Thorne, who was also managing Tone Vale Transport, became a director of Solent, and when Fossett died in 1982 Ken had to spend much of his time with Solent in Southampton rather than in Somerset. Solent also used the workshop in Wiveliscombe for the maintenance of its vehicles, which was an unusual arrangement given the distance between the operations. Travelling to and from a workshop for routine inspections or repairs is dead mileage and therefore uneconomic.

The only major decision Price and Pierce made concerning its new subsidiary during its two-year ownership was to sell Taunton Meat Haulage's site in Bathpool, some two miles from Taunton, and locate the business in a rented warehouse on a former army camp the other side of the town. They left Philip Langdon in charge to carry on much as before, with Thorne in Wiveliscombe (or Southampton) and Tom Hewett in Taunton.

In 1976 Price and Pierce was taken over by another conglomerate called Tozer, Kemsley and Millbourn (TKM). TKM had a weak balance sheet and relied for survival mainly on its valuable concession to sell German-built BMW cars in England. It also owned other transport companies, of which two operated in France, and Smedleys, a vegetable processing company in Spalding, Lincolnshire. TKM told Smedleys to use Langdons as its haulier and instructed Langdons to open a depot in Spalding to service Smedleys. Very few subsidiaries of a conglomerate like being compelled by the parent to use the products or services of a sister company rather than buy on the open market. The Spalding operation always lost money for Langdons, due to its distance from base and the poor quality of the vehicles they had available. The divorce between Langdons and Smedleys took place as soon as TKM sold Langdons.

TKM knew there was no future for the Langdons companies so long as they continued to offer no more than a freight service for full loads from one place to another (known as 'selling wheels'). Anyone with a tractor and a trailer can do that, and the market is fiercely competitive. If the haulier stores goods for the customer as well as carrying them, the business is less easy to move to a competitor. Running a store where there is little movement of goods in and out is not ideal, because the greater profit comes from the handling and the carriage, but it is better than just selling wheels. The best trading conditions occur when throughput is high because pallets are delivered to a store, sorted, and reloaded without being put on racks, a process known as cross-docking.

With the unions still untamed, especially in the docks and the printing industry, those whose trade relied on a supply of paper found it necessary, and costly, to maintain under their own control and away from the ports' stores two- and three-ton rolls of newsprint or other paper, so that when one of the periodic strikes occurred they could stay in business. Tone Vale Transport had done haulage for the Wansborough Paper Company in Watchet and it was a logical extension of that trade to rent a shed at the former army camp and store reels of paper for Wansborough in Taunton. The Finnish company Varma, which is a major supplier to the newspaper industry, also wanted a reserve store of reels of newsprint, and Philip Langdon agreed to keep it for them in a warehouse in Bristol. He also took on business from ICI for the storage and distribution of agricultural fertiliser, which required another shed at the former camp.

The warehouse to be used for the storage of paper at Arnos Castle in Bristol was newly built. Langdon Industries Ltd, as the company was now called, took it over on a 25-year lease. It also took a lease on the same terms of an adjoining newly built warehouse, and TKM lent it £150,000 to convert this second warehouse into a cold store. As was usual with such leases, the rent was reviewed every five years, with revisions only upwards. The ICI fertiliser store in Taunton was also taken on a term lease, but Varma, Wansborough and ICI never gave Langdons a contract for haulage and storage other than on an *ad hoc* basis. It was an example, in the warehousing business, of the banking error of borrowing short and lending long. The consequences of leasing these, and two other, warehouses on such risky terms will be revealed in due course.

1980 was a momentous year for both TKM and Langdons. TKM lost the BMW franchise and, having announced his wish to retire, Philip Langdon was told to recruit a Managing Director. We need to look at these events separately.

BMW had started life building British-designed Austin 7 cars in Germany under licence and had prospered after the Second World War in inverse proportion to Austin's long decline, which had landed it eventually in the ill-starred British Leyland consortium. After losing the BMW franchise, TKM's subsidiary, Wadham Stringer, continued to act as a distributor for British Leyland and remained profitable until 1982, although, with a falling demand for British Leyland vehicles, TKM's finances became increasingly precarious. In March 1981, before major capital expenditure was forbidden, Langdons bought the freehold of a former government sugar storage facility at Walford Cross, midway between Taunton and Bridgwater, to which they moved their

3 *The Langdons' senior management in 1980: from left to right, Tom Hewett, Philip Langdon, Ken Thorne and Michael Donoghue.*

workshop, offices and much of the Wansborough paper. The new Managing Director was also allowed, against Philip Langdon's advice, to convert 10 flat-bed trailers to curtain-sided vehicles, and to buy five temperature-controlled trailers, each with a carrying capacity of 18 pallets.

The only other capital expenditure made by Langdons under TKM ownership was the purchase of 22 rigid lorries with refrigerated bodies from a firm on the Somerset/Wiltshire border called A.G. Maidment and Sons, whose owner wished to retire. An attraction was the fact that Maidment hauled for a major abattoir at Fareham in Hampshire and, to retain the business, Langdons sent a young man called Rupert Ryall to open a depot there. On the downside, the Maidment fleet was a miscellany of old trucks, of six different types, which made the holding of spares for maintenance difficult and costly. Fareham is a long way from Taunton and remote operations, without proper on-site facilities, are rarely profitable. Fareham was no exception.

After 1983 TKM became ever more short of cash. As early as 1981, a year during which Langdons lost money trading, its parent augmented the deficit by extracting a further £45,000 in 'management fees'. Overall Langdons had achieved a small profit in the years since Philip Langdon had sold it, but at the cost of eating the seed corn: rented premises, owner-drivers, hired trailers, non-replacement of obsolescent equipment, risky long-term commitments without contract cover and so on. As its own cash problems grew, TKM compelled Langdons to use its overdraft facility with a Taunton bank to the full and remit any spare cash to headquarters. Eventually TKM was only saved from failure through an injection of cash by the New Zealand tycoon, Ron Brierley, who took control of its operations.

The Managing Director chosen by Philip Langdon was a 33-year-old Scot called Michael Donoghue and it was a decision for which he has to be congratulated. Michael's father had owned a substantial wholesale grocery business in Edinburgh which he still managed after selling to a larger company. Michael had left school at the age of 17 then worked in the same industry as his father, managing a grocery shop, supervising a large cash-and-carry operation, running a cold store, and then becoming a very youthful General Manager of the Transport Division of the substantial Swedish-owned company Frigoscandia. He not only knew every aspect of the temperature-controlled distribution business, everyone in the industry knew him.

Investors rightly frown upon the practice of a Chief Executive becoming Chairman of a company to which a successor has been appointed. The Chairman will have a closer relationship with the staff, and know the background of the business better, than his successor. Striking the right balance is almost impossible: he is likely either to interfere too much or become too remote. Philip Langdon interfered too much, not appreciating that a non-executive Chairman should be ever-available but not ever-present.

Philip retained his own office, which was grander than the accommodation in the warehouse he allocated to Michael. He also continued to consult with the staff on executive matters, and especially with Ken Thorne, although less with the other manager, Tom Hewett. He openly criticised Michael's decisions and then took to writing to TKM with his complaints. That may indeed have been the prerogative of a Chairman unhappy about the performance of his Managing Director, but it is best done other than by dictating the letters to the Managing Director's secretary. Faced with a choice between their Chairman and their Managing Director, TKM eventually told Philip to keep away from the business pending his retirement in May 1983. His last visit to Michael's office at Walford Cross was an unhappy event and a carpenter had to be summoned to repair the door which he slammed in his rage as he left.

Tom Hewett was due to retire in 1984. Ken Thorne had been absent from work suffering from a long illness, possibly caused in part by the invidious position in which he found himself as a loyal servant of Philip Langdon, a director of Solent and manager of the Langdons' ambient haulage and distribution business. On his return, without consulting Michael, he ordered 10 new Volvo trucks which Langdons needed but would have been unable to pay for. Michael was able to cancel the order, citing Ken's illness as an excuse, and Ken left Langdons.

The new Managing Director had other senior vacancies to fill. It transpired that Philip Langdon had in the past promised both Ken Thorne and the company's accountant, Roy Hutchings, that each of them would be appointed

4 *Langdons' Fleet in 1956.*

Managing Director when he retired. Apart from Philip's unfulfilled promise, Roy thought, as able accountants often do, that he had been the right man for the job, and left the company. In 1985 Roy's equally competent successor, Bill Wallace, also left. Apart from losing accountants, with the retirement of Tom Hewett and the departure of Ken Thorne Michael's pressing need was to find an Operations Manager. Here he was fortunate to recruit a 32-year-old man called Rob Swindells, whose career in transport had been as varied and instructive as his own.

Rob Swindells had been unable to take up a university place due to family financial problems. He worked first as a van driver, and then drove Heavy Goods Vehicles with a Class I licence. After two years on the road, much of it on the continent, he took a salary cut and a job as a trainee traffic manager in the Transport Development Group (TDG), a large and well-run haulage and distribution company. Like Michael Donoghue, Rob knew the business from the bottom up, and the drivers knew that he knew it.

Once they had been given a chance to show their worth, Michael found that within Langdons there were a number of loyal and competent managers: Paul Rowe, Glan Robottom and David Every-Clayton in administration and finance; Trevor Horton in the workshops; Chris Murt and Dorothy Brown (now Stone), who had run the Avonmouth operation; Rupert Ryall at Fareham; Sheila Burnett and Jackie Hampton in the office; and drivers like Derek Champion, Ron Blake, Gordon Ardren, Peter Langdon and Maxi Mehrlich, whose ability Michael recognised and respected. These people were to help him transform the company.

In the year to December 1983, under Michael and his team, Langdons seemed to have turned the corner, making a profit of £60,000 before management fees to TKM. That year TKM sold another of its transport companies, Laser Transport, to its managers, but Michael's request to make an offer for Langdons was rejected because TKM said it could not afford to sell such a profitable subsidiary. Appearances were, as so often, deceptive. Langdons desperately needed investment in new equipment if it was to survive. It could not even afford to buy racking for its warehouses, which severely restricted the types of storage and distribution business for which it could bid. When Ron Brierley took control he was more pragmatic. Two years later, after protracted negotiations which we will look at in some detail, Michael Donoghue, Rob Swindells and Paul Rowe were to buy Langdons.

Our lessons from the above can be summarised as follow:

- Operating old equipment is a false economy.
- Restrict your vehicle types so as to economise on spare parts in stock-holding.
- Have your repair shop near your main base to prevent dead running.
- Avoid setting up remote depots without administration and back-up facilities.
- Do not compel subsidiary sister companies to trade exclusively with each other.
- Keep up with new technology.
- Do not allow individuals to place orders for equipment without full consultation and insist on the use of numbered order forms.
- Recruit or train able and experienced managers and support them.
- Don't take on long-term commitments backed by short-term contracts.
- When you retire as Chief Executive Officer, keep out of your successor's way.

Chapter 4

TKM SELL LANGDONS TO THE MANAGEMENT

The profit in 1983 was followed by heavy losses in the first eight months of 1984. This was not a ploy by Michael Donoghue to persuade TKM to come back to him about a sale. The various adverse factors to which we have already referred were combining to make a return to profitability unlikely. First there were the interest payments on the bank overdraft, with much of the borrowed money having been siphoned off by TKM rather than used in Langdons to renew equipment. Next there were the high rents paid for the leased properties in Bristol and in Taunton, with only the freehold warehouse at Walford Cross, the ICI shed and the controlled-temperature store in Arnos Castle showing a profit. The four remote operations, in London, Manchester, Spalding and Fareham, were all losing money. Because of poor equipment both on the road and in the warehouses, the firm was limited to bidding for the lowest margin types of work. Then there were the owner-drivers.

In theory, an owner-driver will be more motivated than a company employee and less likely to maltreat a tractor which is his own property, although even the best of them prefer to wear out the firm's trailer brakes than those on their tractor. All, however, are likely to be selective about the work they are given and unhappy about making the inevitable unprofitable journeys. The more successful tend eventually to leave and set up their own businesses.

Langdons kept the accounts for its owner-drivers, also acting as their banker by collecting their revenue and paying their bills. When an account moved into credit, it was understandable that the driver wanted to withdraw the surplus cash for personal expenditure rather than build up a reserve for future contingencies. To conserve his money, he might be reluctant to contribute towards the cost of a new tractor, especially if he could arrange a loan which Langdons would have to guarantee, though old vehicles are unreliable and costly to maintain, and when a major repair was needed Langdons usually had to lend the driver the money to pay for it.

In practice, almost all owner-driver accounts were permanently in debit, funded by the company. In the 19 months to October 1984, Langdons had to write off £47,000 against these unrecoverable debts. This was not a book figure; it was cash paid out and lost. The company could not afford to dispense with the owner-drivers because by then it only operated two articulated tractors driven by employees, apart from the three old dogs which were unlicensed and used as shunters. But it could not survive if it had to continue funding the owner-drivers at that rate.

Before Michael Donoghue approached TKM in 1983 about their selling him the business, he knew that he needed advice. Doing a Management Buy-Out (MBO) is like buying a house: you don't do it very often, it is a complex process, and you need help from someone who knows how to set about it. Michael's next-door neighbour, Gordon Copley, worked for a management recruitment office in Bristol which was the branch of a London firm. The Bristol office was managed by John Henderson, with whom I had worked over the years since we first met when I was buying a small company from Rolls Royce in the dark days of its receivership. After the London office of Henderson's company ran into financial difficulties, I had for two years helped nurse it back to health.

I had another connection with John Henderson. When my family and I formed a company called West Monkton Advisory Services (WMAS) to help troubled firms, its registered office was at his offices in Bristol so that its tax affairs would be handled by an Inspector more experienced than the one in Taunton. To complete the picture, Gordon Copley's son, one of Michael's step-sons and one of my sons were in the same form at school.

In the two decades or so in which I, and then WMAS, had been involved in corporate rescues and MBOs, we had developed mutual confidence with the Chairman of a merchant bank called Richard Cox-Johnson, with the Regional Directors of joint-stock banks, including Peter Dobbs at Lloyds, with accountants of the calibre of Tom Allen, a senior partner in Peats, and with investors such as The Growth Fund, which was then advised by Charles Breese. We had access to pension experts, who would assess potential liabilities, and the bankers knew that we would advise buyers not to give personal guarantees for company borrowings: if the deal wasn't good enough to stand on its own, you shouldn't do it.

The traffic with bankers and the like was not all one way. There are occasions where a bank or Development Agency finds belatedly that it has lent a business too much money and cannot afford to put in a receiver. They may then ask someone like WMAS to have a look at the problem and stay with the borrower to help recover the situation by showing the company how to trade out of its difficulties.

Lenders to MBOs usually accepted a business plan drawn up by WMAS working with the company management, especially if WMAS were willing to make an equity investment in the company on the same terms as other outsiders. We were able to keep the costs down because the family included chartered accountants and solicitors, and we only needed to employ expensive professionals when we knew the deal was going through.

WMAS had no office and no overheads, and because all of us in the family who were involved had other sources of income, it had no full-time employee and no monthly wage bill. It could afford to pick and choose among those who sought its advice, and to charge accordingly or, as with Langdons and others, not at all. It was also, although this is not germane to our story, an effective way of passing assets from one generation to another without troubling the Inland Revenue.

Michael Donoghue appreciated that an employee can be at a disadvantage in any negotiation with his bosses about a buy-out. Apart from the master/servant relationship, it is often necessary to remind the employer of things he would rather not hear, and that is best done by an outsider. After preparing an outline business plan and having preliminary discussions with Richard Cox-Johnson, Michael and I had agreed on what kind of an offer we should make, and I went on 6 April 1983 to meet a director of TKM on my own. Our proposal included the condition that TKM should retain the Arnos Castle properties in Bristol, not just because of the liability under the leases but because some £180,000 was outstanding on the conversion of one of the warehouses to a cold store. TKM were unhappy about keeping the properties and also thought our offer was £150,000 too low, and a week later they rejected it.

As a vendor may remain liable for the debts of a company it sells for 12 months after the deal, to prevent fraud by disposing of liabilities to a man of straw it is normal to reveal your business plan when you make the bid. TKM were sufficiently impressed by ours to offer WMAS the job of preparing business plans for all their transport companies, which was not a good idea. You cannot serve God and Mammon. They then commissioned a consultant to report on Langdons. The advice they received in October 1984 was not unwise but it was impracticable – dispose of Arnos Castle, invest in new equipment, relocate from Taunton to Bristol or Exeter to secure outward traffic, and so on. Nobody wanted the onerous leases; there was no money for new equipment: a move would also cost money.

By this time TKM, under Brierley's ownership, had appointed a Disposals Manager who hawked Langdons round its competitors without success before, on 29 November 1984, asking Michael Donoghue to make another offer. Michael and I saw him with Langdons' accountant, Bill Wallace, on 14 January 1985 and suggested a figure which was substantially less than what we had proposed in April 1983. The Disposals Manager was unhappy that an outsider such as I was should have been at the meeting, and showed his annoyance by being rather rude to me. Bill Wallace was so depressed by the TKM attitude that he decided take a job elsewhere.

By the summer of 1985 Langdons was beginning to lose serious money. On 27 September, faced with unacceptable closure and redundancy costs, TKM again asked Michael to make a bid. Two months later we returned with an offer which was £500,000 less than their previous asking price, although we did agree to keep the onerous Arnos Castle leases. This time I dealt one-to-one with TKM's Managing Director, who was helpful and realistic, and we completed the deal on 2 April 1986, with the transfer backdated to 1 January.

The buy-out involved around £1 million of assets (including the freehold site at Walford Cross) for which we were paying £750,000. TKM received £8,000 in cash and agreed to leave £150,000 on loan as well as the further balance of £150,000 outstanding on the conversion of the Arnos Castle chill store, both to be repaid over a period without interest. There was a hiatus at

5 *The buy-out team from an early brochure.*

the last moment when the Growth Fund, which had agreed to take both shares and loan capital, decided not to participate because one of its partners, UK Provident, ran into difficulties with the authorities over its liquidity ratio, and finding £250,000 over the Easter holiday was only possible because Richard Cox-Johnson, Charles Breese and others agreed to make up most of the deficit out of their own pockets, leaving a shortfall of £45,000, which WMAS introduced over and above its agreed 14 per cent share.

Peter Dobbs at Lloyds Bank provided a term loan of £250,000 and an overdraft facility. More important was his arrangement to provide £1.4 million to allow owner-drivers to buy new tractors on terms which were not penal. The task now was to put our business plan into effect and turn a loss of £300,000 in 1985 into a profit of £150,000 in 1986. But before we look at the plan, how it was constructed and how it was implemented, let us consider what lessons there may be for anyone considering an MBO.

- Get independent advice from a third party on any MBO.
- Do not try to do a deal with your boss on your own.
- Use an adviser who is prepared to stay with the business and help implement any business plan.
- Take your time. Do not allow yourself to be rushed into any deal.
- Beware long leases or other ongoing commitments and pension liabilities.
- Stay clear of owner-driver schemes.
- Try to avoid giving bankers any personal guarantee.

Chapter 5

CARRYING OUT THE BUSINESS PLAN

There is nothing secret or clever about identifying the problems of a loss-making business because, as I pointed out in *Thinking About Management*, first published in 1992, there are only four things you can do to reduce losses or increase profits. The options are to increase prices without losing sales; to increase volume without increasing fixed costs; to reduce fixed or variable costs without losing volume; or to get out of the business. In practice a recovery plan normally involves elements of all four options. Specifying the actions to be taken by a firm is the easy part. Implementation is more difficult because it almost always involves cost reductions and, as the adage goes, costs walk on two legs.

The simplest and least painful route to increase profit or remain solvent is to increase prices without losing sales. This is how local authorities and other state monopolies operate, which is why council taxes increase year on year at rates in excess of inflation and why the National Health Service needs more and more cash without any corresponding increase in efficiency or performance. All the other options involve dismissing people or making them work more efficiently, and that is seldom pleasant for a manager to deal with and therefore avoided when there is a softer option. Politicians, councillors and those they employ are not spending their own money and the public businesses they run cannot go bankrupt. In the private sector, managers are spending their own money or that of their shareholders, and their firms can go bankrupt.

With Langdons, at the time of the MBO in 1986 arbitrary price increases were not an option. The company had no unique selling proposition or other competitive advantages such as a favourable location or superior facilities. If it increased prices it would risk losing what profitable business it had.

Langdons was also unable to increase volume without increasing fixed costs in its transport and warehousing facilities, because its rented warehouses lacked pallet-racking and were full of goods being stored at low rates, and its ramshackle fleet was working to capacity given its current customer base. Its most valuable asset was the freehold seven-acre site at Walford Cross adjacent to the junction of two major trunk roads and situated midway between two motorway exits. No fewer than 4,390 heavy goods vehicles used these highways every weekday and drivers are obliged by law to take a periodic rest. They also need a safe and convenient location for overnight parking. Much of the space in the yard was occupied by Langdons' vehicles only at weekends because, with little locally generated outward traffic, they tended to be away from base for most of the week. To get more revenue from the site, Michael Donoghue conceived the brilliant but simple idea of converting the firm's offices into a café and throwing the yard open to other hauliers as a truck stop and bunkering facility. There could have been no better example of increasing sales without increasing fixed costs.

The third option, to reduce costs without losing volume, was applicable only to those parts of the business which Langdons wished and was able to keep. Closing all the bases other than those in Taunton and Bristol saved expense without materially affecting profitable turnover. Rupert Ryall shut down his operation in Fareham and moved to Taunton. The closure of the yards in London and Manchester demonstrated what a waste of money it had been to have opened them in the first place.

The company achieved significant reduction in the cost of its borrowings. As we noted, the £300,000 left by TKM as a debt did not carry interest. A further £375,000 was in share capital, which potentially involved the payment of dividends out of profit, but no interest. That left only the interest-bearing £200,000 which had been advanced by Peter Dobbs at Lloyds Bank, rather than the £540,000 on which Langdons had been paying interest to the Midland Bank before the MBO. It is worth noting that, from the outset, investors were told that Langdons would pay out no more than a quarter of its profits in dividends and it would never borrow in total a sum greater than its equity capital and

6 *The truck stop's bar area.*

reserves. Conservative and cautious policies such as these may inhibit growth but they ensure stability and it is as well to spell them out from the start.

Another important cost reduction was in the use of working capital. Unlike a manufacturing business, transport and distribution involves no work in progress. You provide a service and, in about 45 days, hope to get paid for it. Pending payment you fund the cost of operating the vehicles and warehouses and other overhead expenses. By dropping loss-making operations and halving the annual turnover of the business from £6 million, the company needed £150,000 less working capital after the MBO than it had under TKM, and it was on this calculation that TKM agreed an unsecured loan for that amount, knowing that the cash would be generated within two months of the MBO as the turnover decreased.

The fourth option is to get out of the business. Within days of the MBO, Langdons closed the loss-making Spalding depot and ceased working for Smedleys. The team scrutinised every major account to ensure the work was profitable. For example, the firm's fifth biggest customer was a manufacturer of hardboard located at South Molton, some 45 miles to the west of Walford Cross at the far end of Exmoor. The business did not just involve vehicles running light to pick up the traffic: Langdons also stationed one of its shunters free of charge in the customer's yard to move trailers. The withdrawal of the shunter meant that local hauliers took on the work and Langdons stopped losing money there.

The fuel company Texaco, which took on the franchise for the bunkering facility at Walford Cross, provided the cash for the conversion of the truck stop. Being able to aggregate the volume of fuel bought by visiting drivers with the usage by its own vehicles, Langdons was able to reduce its own fuel bill significantly. Under Paul Rowe's management, the truck stop was profitable from the day it opened, averaging 70 overnight parking customers and another 300 visits each day. The restaurant became popular with car drivers as well as truckers and the bar, though busy in the evenings, never led to excessive drinking. When Texaco ran into financial difficulties due to the problems of its parent company in America, BP took over the fuel franchise, and a fresh injection of capital from them paid for the provision of 14 bedrooms. By then, in addition to the restaurant and bunkering, there was a shop, a snooker room and a hairdressing salon. The water in the showers was always hot and the lavatories were kept clean. In a trade magazine, Walford Cross was voted by lorry drivers as the best truck stop in the country. Its success, however, was to cause an amicable difference of opinion with its supportive shareholder, Richard Cox-Johnson, to which we will refer shortly.

Rob Swindells, you may recall, had been recruited before the MBO as Operations Manager. With the relocation to Walford Cross of depot managers Chris Murt from Avonmouth and Rupert Ryall from Fareham, the company had two experienced and able men to run the ambient and temperature-controlled sides of the business in the traffic office. This allowed Rob to spend more of his time seeking new business. Because he lived in Bristol, he was also able to keep an eye on the warehouses and staff at Arnos Castle, where many of the company vehicles parked overnight, and eventually he worked from an office there, being the first person in the firm to use a word processor rather than a secretary.

Operating costs fell as the owner-drivers bought new tractors using the facility provided by Peter Dobbs at Lloyds. Every breakdown for a haulier is an unbudgeted expense, even if the cargo is at ambient temperature without a shelf life. Temperature-controlled – frozen or chilled – goods may become undeliverable if the tractor or the compressor on the refrigeration plant break down, leading not just to lost revenue but to a claim for damages from the customer. Michael Donoghue was not yet able to start replacing the owner-drivers by company employees, but he could at least see that the owner-drivers drove reliable vehicles.

We noted how Michael had converted 10 flat-bed trailers to curtain-sided before the MBO. Although pallets have to be secured in a curtain-sided trailer, there is none of the sheeting down with ropes and tarpaulins which the driver has to carry out when using a flat-bed, nor is there the same risk of damage to the cargo from bad weather. As funds permitted, Michael sent another 30 flat-beds for conversion, which improved the quality of the fleet and reduced time spent loading and unloading. The five refrigerated trailers he had bought before the MBO carried only 18 pallets, which was then the legal limit. They were also equipped with hooks for conveying hanging meat carcasses. With the regulations under review, he decided not to buy fresh refrigerated trailers but to hire them at spot rates, that is to say, without entering any long-term commitment. In

7 *Stacked paper reels at Arnos Castle warehouse.*

this way, the company was able to match the availability of equipment with customer demand on a weekly basis, albeit at more expense than using contract hire, but without taking on any longer-term commitment.

Another area of fixed cost reduction was in the rented warehousing. One lease expired in Taunton in March 1986 and the new owners were able to throw back the claim by the landlord for dilapidations into the previous year, which meant that it was paid by TKM. The same landlord wished to regain possession of another warehouse for which the lease expired in 1991. Michael Donoghue agreed to release it if the claim for dilapidations were waived. This meant that, apart from the onerous leases at Arnos Castle in Bristol, the company had managed to escape from long-term liabilities on warehouses just as it avoided them on vehicles and equipment.

Such drastic and fundamental changes of direction and management could have proved expensive, but this was not the case. Although, with the shutting of depots, there was a reduction in the number of owner-drivers, very few company employees were made redundant. The outside shareholders, as was reasonable, asked for a qualified accountant to be appointed Finance Director and for a non-executive Chairman. Both of these posts were filled by members of WMAS. In practice, Paul Rowe and David Every-Clayton continued to prepare accounts as they had done prior to the MBO. Michael Donoghue was able to fill posts by redeploying existing staff and it is a tribute to him and to them that most of those he appointed were still with the company twenty years later.

Having made a plan and implemented it, Michael and his team set about developing the business. For most hauliers, the secret to success is return loading, with outward traffic taken for granted. Warehouses are more profitable if they are equipped with racking to facilitate the stacking and storage of pallets by fork-lift trucks; this results in constant movement of goods in and out, and revenue from cross-docking. Langdons would remain at a competitive disadvantage so long as it lacked outward traffic from Taunton and continued to operate unracked warehouses. It would be some time before Michael could afford to buy the racking, but seeking locally generated work cost nothing and we will see how he and Rob Swindells addressed the problem, so cutting out excessive and wasteful mileage by unladen vehicles.

To summarise the lessons learnt:

- Nothing in the business world ever stands still. Remember the four things you can do to improve profitability.
- Think laterally.
- Redeploy and retrain staff where possible rather than dismiss or recruit.
- Do not use working overdraft facilities for capital projects.
- Avoid excessive borrowing and over-gearing.
- Agree financial rules and stick to them.
- Buy the best equipment you can afford.

Chapter 6
RE-ALIGNING THE BUSINESS IN A CHANGING ENVIRONMENT

We saw how the new management at Langdons in effect abandoned the plasterboard traffic from South Molton because of the empty running involved. At the time of the MBO the company retained two ambient accounts which were more satisfactory, both involving inwards carriage to a warehouse and then delivery to the eventual customers. One of these related to nitrates for agricultural use carried in intermediate bulk containers (IBCs) – those large square non-returnable floppy bags holding half a ton or more of powder. The warehousing did not require racking as the bags could be piled on top of each other without causing damage. Langdons sometimes collected the IBCs from a chemical plant in Immingham on Humberside and carried them to Taunton. It stored them, and then distributed them to farms in the West Country. The customer was ICI and the business had every good quality – inward and outward traffic, warehousing, and a customer who paid bills on time without constantly carping about the cost. The only problem was that agricultural use of nitrates damages the water table, and for that reason less nitrates were being sold as artificial fertiliser to farmers.

The other key account involved the two- and three-ton rolls of newsprint and other paper which Langdons received, sometimes in containers, at Walford Cross, at another store in Taunton and in Arnos Castle. As with the IBCs, these rolls could be stacked on top of each other, to perilous heights, and needed no racking. While the inward traffic in containers from the docks was done by other hauliers, there was regular outward business from both Taunton and Bristol, until the reforms cautiously introduced by Mrs Thatcher made it unnecessary for bulk users of paper to hold reserve supplies against frequent and unpredictable strikes by dockers. As the need to store reserve stocks of paper diminished, so the business contracted and the regular outward traffic from Taunton and Bristol was lost.

Three large manufacturing concerns were potential sources of regular and significant outward ambient traffic from the Taunton area. One was Taunton Cider, situated at Norton Fitzwarren, some two miles out of Taunton. Another was Gerber Foods, which processed imported fruit juice in Bridgwater for supermarket own labels. The third was Relyon, the bed manufacturer at Wellington, about 10 miles from Walford Cross, which had developed fireproof foam widely used by other furniture manufacturers. Michael Donoghue and Rob Swindells were determined to secure business from all three of these potential customers.

At the time of the MBO in 1986 Taunton Cider was owned by a consortium of brewers with whom it enjoyed exclusive supply agreements. The business had started with the sale of the delicious cider produced by the Rectors of Heathfield, near Norton Fitzwarren, whose glebe included an orchard of Kingston Black apples. The first surviving receipt for the ecclesiastical cider is dated June 1842, and by 1910 the Rector, the Revd Edward Spurway, was overseeing the production of 5,000 gallons of cider a year, which was delivered by rail to the great and the good throughout the land. In 1912 Spurway fell ill and his successor to the benefice, conscious no doubt of the evils of the demon drink, sold the business and orchards to a local builder. After various vicissitudes, in 1965 Miles Roberts had been appointed Managing Director and forged links with leading brewers both as shareholders and customers. By 1970 this policy resulted in the firm producing 4.7 million gallons of cider a year.

Although Taunton Cider operated its own fleet of 16 articulated units, the increase in the turnover from £57.5 to £109.4 million between 1988 and 1991 meant it had plenty of business to place with outside hauliers. Handling the account personally, Michael Donoghue secured Langdons' pre-eminence as its preferred, and most reliable, supplier of transport. Looking ahead, the Langdons' business with Taunton Cider grew year on year and by 1995 was worth £1,255,441. So close had the working partnership become that the two companies then agreed in principal for Langdons to take over all of Taunton Cider's warehousing operations as well as its transport.

The second prospect, Gerber Foods, had acquired a small Bridgwater company called Quantock Jams, for which Langdons had in the past done some storage. Although Rob Swindells enjoyed a cordial relationship with the Gerber management, he was unable to obtain any transport work because that was performed by a Bridgwater firm which had both the requisite vehicles and warehouses. As we shall see, keeping in touch proved of great value when Gerber Foods started producing chilled fruit juices and its Bridgwater haulier

8   *Taunton Cider Ltd before the war.*

was unwilling or unable to offer the requisite temperature-controlled vehicles and storage space.

The third prospect in the Taunton area, Relyon, was a difficult customer because Langdons' vehicles were not configured to carry lightweight bulk such as the flameproof foam material, nor were its drivers adept in the delicate task of handling mattresses wrapped in cellophane. After Michael Donoghue had won the business of delivering foam the two companies maintained a friendly but uneasy relationship, the only hard words spoken being when Langdons moved out of ambient transport, leaving Relyon to find another haulier.

With more locally generated traffic, and less running light, the ambient fleet became profitable, albeit with a low margin. But so long as Langdons could only offer to carry full loads from point to point it would meet intense competition both from bigger national firms with fixed contracts and from smaller businesses operating on lower overheads. Without rigid vehicles for individual pallet deliveries, and racked warehousing space to offer customers a picking service, it would remain at a commercial disadvantage.

Just as the paper business and nitrate businesses were falling away, so Langdons' temperature-controlled activities were under threat. As we noted, its refrigerated trailers were fitted with meat hooks to carry carcasses from the abattoir to the butcher. With more meat being supplied to supermarkets, abattoirs were carrying out the jointing and packing of meat rather than selling the carcasses, which meant that, instead of hanging inside the trailer, the meat tended to be shrink-wrapped and palletised. Langdons' trailers were less suited for this haulage and the company had no temperature-controlled warehouse in which loads could be stored and picked for eventual delivery. This was a serious drawback because, unlike ambient stores where goods can remain for indefinite periods, in refrigerated stores there is constant stock movement and cross-docking revenue.

Despite gaining outward temperature-controlled business from a dairy at Hemyock in East Devon and meat from Chard, by 1990 Langdons was considering withdrawing altogether from refrigerated haulage. Its 18-pallet trailers equipped with meat hooks were obsolescent. It could only haul a full trailer-load from one destination to another because it was unable to offer intermediate storage and picking facilities, 'picking' being the making up of an order on a single pallet from buffer stock held in the store. It had no regular access, or slots for delivery, to the Regional Distribution Centres (RDCs) of the supermarkets. By contrast, its ambient work with Taunton Cider and other regular customers was growing rapidly and the fleet was achieving better return loading factors. Even in Bristol the carriage of plasterboard from Avonmouth had replaced the lost paper trade. There was one other important account, involving the delivery of the soft drinks Ribena and Lucozade for SmithKlineBeecham from Coleford in the Forest of Dean.

To get to Coleford from Bristol you have to cross the River Severn, which involves not just a long drive but also paying a toll. In 1987 a garage with a café and large yard came up for sale on the trunk road between Ross-on-Wye and

Monmouth, not far from Coleford. Encouraged by the success of the truck stop at Walford Cross, and aware of the obstacles to the rapid growth facing the transport and warehousing business, Richard Cox-Johnson was anxious that Langdons should concentrate on opening truck stops rather than on developing transport and distribution, and was confident that such a policy could be financed. The manager/shareholders were less sure. There would indeed be advantages in having a depot near Coleford, but it would become a liability if the company lost the Ribena and Lucozade business. The Walford Cross truck stop was so profitable because it operated out of an existing facility which was already carrying most of the fixed overheads. And, anyway, Langdons was primarily a transport business.

In 1986 Richard and others had at short notice invested their own money to enable the MBO to proceed. All venture capitalists, except perhaps 3is, tend to be short-term investors, looking for a quick exit and profit so that they can move on to the next deal. Faced with the difference of opinion with the management over the future direction the business should take, Richard and some of the outside investors indicated in 1988 that they would like to sell out.

Although the 1985 losses had turned into profit, the company was in no position to buy in some £300,000 of shares, nor were the MBO team prepared to agree to selling Langdons to a competitor. Faced with an impasse, WMAS came up with the scheme that Michael Donoghue, Paul Rowe and Rob Swindells should leave Langdons' employment, form a management company, and sell their services to Langdons. Although the auditors frowned on the idea, fearing that what was proposed might contravene company law, Peter Dobbs at Lloyds Bank was, as ever, supportive, providing the management company with funds to buy out Richard Cox-Johnson and the other outside shareholders and even paying them a premium of 50 per cent to reward them for their participation. And so, by 1988, the four original MBO team gained total control of Langdons and reverted to its agreed shareholding whereby Michael Donoghue controlled just under half the business, Paul Rowe and Rob Swindells had 18 per cent each, and WMAS owned 14 per cent.

The management were still vacillating about the future of its struggling temperature-controlled operation in November 1990 when a newspaper report gave hope of escaping from Arnos Castle and, in the process, generating funds to develop its warehouses, and that is where we look next.

- Business is constantly changing and evolving. Think ahead.
- Identify key sales prospects and devote your best resources to developing them.
- Keep your banker informed about the business and pass on bad news as well as good.
- Remember that venture capitalists look for an early exit.
- Keep in contact with a prospective customer even if you get no orders.
- Concentrate on your core business and avoid distractions.

Chapter 7

THE REVIVAL OF REFRIGERATION

The 18th September 1989 was a sad day because it was then that I went to the farewell lunch given to Peter Dobbs in Salisbury on his retirement as Regional Director and General Manager of Lloyds Bank. I was glad to have been asked to propose his health. He had been resolute in his support for Langdons and wise in the advice he had given us. I also had cause to remember that day because I, and several other people, saw two youths engaged in a criminal activity. As the others went about their business, I asked the car park attendant to call the police. From the information I was able to give, the youths were later arrested and the police asked me to attend an identification parade the next day, involving the loss of a morning's work and a drive of 130 miles. When I reached Salisbury, so straitened were the resources of the Wiltshire Constabulary that no officer was available to hold the parade or even to take a statement from me. Four years later, as we will see, this manpower shortage seems to have been remedied. The two criminals later pleaded guilty.

In 1990 Gerber Foods in Bridgwater introduced two new lines of fruit juice, kept chilled rather than at ambient temperature. As their existing haulier had no refrigerated vehicles, Langdons took on the transport. Gerber lacked facilities for 'picking', or selecting product in a store as ordered by a customer and putting it on pallets for delivery, and so Langdons' vehicles were frequently held up while Gerber's staff were scratching around to fill an order. To compound the problem, production scheduling frequently meant that there was insufficient of the requisite product available, leading to short deliveries. The solution was for Langdons to establish a chilled store to which all the production could be sent direct from the Bridgwater factory. Langdons could then hold intermediate stocks from which orders could be picked and dispatched.

With the decline in the paper business Langdons had plenty of space at Walford Cross, but the conversion of part of it to a chilled store was estimated to cost £275,000. The company would not have broken its rule that borrowings should never exceed its equity by accepting a loan of that size, but Lloyds Bank, without the experienced Peter Dobbs managing the account and smarting from losses incurred in connection with the failure of another privately owned transport firm, declined to advance the money.

Meanwhile, in Bristol the government had established a Development Corporation to revive a derelict part of the city, and this work necessitated the demolition of the warehouses at Arnos Castle. We will look in due course at the negotiations which Michael Donoghue handled because there are lessons to be learned. Here it is relevant to note that the compensation paid for the disturbance of the tenant, Tom Granby Ltd, from the refrigerated warehouse amounted to £275,000, or precisely the amount of money needed to convert part of the Walford Cross warehouse from ambient to temperature-controlled. Fortunately Tom Granby, whose Managing Director was the able and amiable Michael Redmond, had no wish to relocate in Taunton and found new premises in Bristol without needing any financial inducement.

Converting the warehouse by insulating it and controlling its temperature was only part of the problem. To operate the store, Langdons needed to install racking, which is also costly. Again the bank demurred about lending the money, whereupon Michael Donoghue and WMAS brought out their own wallets. As shareholders' loans are deferred in any receivership, this demonstrated both their confidence in the company and in the future of its relationship with Gerber. Lloyds Bank, after recovering its nerve, was to appoint a series of able business managers to handle the Langdons' account and never again hesitated in providing whatever finance the company required.

The new facility at Walford Cross was far from perfect because at the start there were only two loading bays. That would have been no great liability with ambient goods, but with chilled or frozen product it is necessary for the trailer or rigid lorry to be backed snugly up to the ramp to maintain the requisite temperature. Once a pallet has been filled, it has to be stretch-wrapped, which serves two functions. The wrapping contains the load and it deters pilferage.

9 *Christopher Murt (left) and Trevor Horton (right).*

In the early days the job at Langdons had to be performed laboriously by hand because luxuries such as automatic stretch-wrapping equipment had to wait.

Virtually all the chilled Gerber fruit juice went to supermarkets, which in most cases do not accept deliveries from suppliers to individual stores but concentrate them in their Regional Distribution Centres (RDCs). A driver cannot just turn up with goods at an RDC and expect to be unloaded, or 'tipped' in the vernacular, because of necessity the RDCs ration access to their loading bays. The haulier is given a delivery time and, although some leeway has to be allowed for traffic conditions, late arrivals may find themselves turned away, especially if the supermarket has over-ordered or is already fully stocked. Inevitably not every trailer carrying Gerber product to an RDC was full, and Langdons therefore had the opportunity to piggyback smaller loads for other customers to the RDCs, using the delivery slots allotted for Gerber's fruit juice. Although Gerber paid by the pallet rather than the load, delivery had to be made even if the trailer had spare capacity, and this surplus space, effectively already paid for, allowed Rob Swindells to offer customers not just access to the RDCs but also access at competitive prices.

The warehouse staff at Walford Cross had some previous experience in picking because a Dorset firm which distributed marine equipment manufactured at Ålesund in Norway had contracted for Langdons to do the warehousing and distribution using the store. Although it lacked adequate facilities, Langdons had secured this business through its connection with WMAS. (Many years previously WMAS had also answered a call for help from the Norwegian company when it had found itself in financial difficulty. Its problem had been so basic and easily rectified that, having recovered the air fare and hotel bill, WMAS waived any fee. We must never forget the debt we owe the Norwegian people for their courage in the Second World War and none were braver than those in Ålesund, one of the ports from which the Shetland Bus operated throughout the German occupation, carrying refugees one way and Norwegian resistance fighters and spies the other.)

Langdons were fortunate to discover that Chris Murt, its senior traffic controller, had a genius for storekeeping. Given the most confused situation and untrained staff, within days Chris could restore order from chaos and leave behind him an operation where the systems worked and those operating them had full confidence in their own skills. Unfortunately, Chris did not have the ability to be in two places at once, and when he was sorting out a store with total concentration and commitment he left a huge gap in the traffic office.

While the Gerber work was developing, Langdons participated in a venture called Palletways, which had been set up by a firm near Lichfield in the heart of England. Each haulier who was involved received the exclusive right to collect and deliver pallets in its allocated postal district. The collected pallets were taken to a single hangar in the Midlands where they were sorted and the vehicle returned loaded for local delivery. The ability to offer a standard single pallet rate for the whole country was an important innovation even if it involved unnecessary mileage through there only being one hub. A pallet from Exeter for delivery in Taunton, for example, might be carried by the Exeter haulier to Lichfield before being taken back to Taunton by Langdons.

In 1990 there was no equivalent service available for chilled or sub-zero traffic. Chilled goods have to be kept at a temperature between 1 and 5 degrees, while sub-zero have to be at anything around minus 20 degrees. This means that chilled and sub-zero goods cannot be kept in the same store nor can they be transported in the same compartment of a vehicle. Having handed over his duties as Operations Director to Chris Murt so that he could concentrate on selling, Rob Swindells especially was keenly aware that there was no facility for the nation-wide fixed-rate delivery of individual pallets of temperature-controlled goods similar to that developed by Palletways. There is, however, a wide gulf between identifying a market opportunity and having the resources to exploit it. For the moment, Langdons saw the opportunity but lacked the resources.

Meanwhile, the firm remained on good terms with its former tenant at Arnos Castle, Tom Granby, for whom Michael Redmond had developed a business storing and delivering temperature-controlled goods based on warehouses in Knowlsey near Liverpool, in Bristol and at Luton. Tom Granby also delivered ambient goods and one of its main contracts was with Rail Gourmet, supplying sandwiches and other foodstuffs and drinks stores to each of 35 mainline railway stations throughout the country on a daily basis. Tom Granby was owned by a German company with an office in Dublin and Michael Redmond seemed to be denied the resources which he needed for the expansion of his business. Although he leased adequate numbers of rigid vehicles for local deliveries, he needed help in trunking articulated loads between some of his depots. This was ideal work for Langdons and another step towards its becoming a national rather than a regional haulier.

By 1995 Langdons was growing as fast as it could given its self-imposed borrowing limits. Apart from its work for Taunton Cider, the Bristol plasterboard manufacturer Lafarge was pressing it for more and more vehicles. Michael Donoghue and his team saw many opportunities but there was a limit to how many of them they could grasp. A major constraint concerned the availability of equipment, and that is something we need to consider next.

- Set a long-term goal and work towards it.
- Even if you rely on a single source of finance, check alternatives.
- Only lend a company your own money as a director if you are confident you will recover it.
- Use an expert to organise and train your storekeepers.
- Stretch-wrap loads on pallets.

Chapter 8

FINANCING IMPROVEMENTS IN THE FLEET

For a number of reasons which we will consider later, Langdons rarely looked outside its existing personnel for senior managerial appointments. There came a time, however, when Paul Rowe was so occupied with the truck stop and the supervision of owner-drivers, among other things, that he was unable to give much assistance to David Every-Clayton with the accounts; nor was Rob Holder, the member of WMAS who had been appointed Finance Director at the time of the MBO, available to do the job in fact as well as in name. Appointees from outside proved a disappointment until, as we will see, Simon Holder, another member of WMAS, was able to devote the necessary hours to the job on a part-time basis. Simon also worked closely with Michael Donoghue on commercial policy, acting as his sounding board after Michael became Chairman in 2000.

Trevor Horton, who managed the workshop, had learned his trade as an apprentice with Tone Vale Transport in Wiveliscombe. No company could have enjoyed the services of a more committed and knowledgeable mechanical engineer than Trevor, but, as with David Every-Clayton and the accounts, when the business grew, Trevor couldn't do everything. The company then secured the services on a part-time basis of Barrie Hargreaves, a retired marine Chief Engineer and, like most men who have spent their life at sea, a man of great experience, unflappability and resource. When Barrie retired he was replaced in 1999 by the unassuming but extremely competent Graham Millard, who had been working in a similar capacity for a haulage subsidiary of BOC.

Michael Donoghue, you may recall, had been a youthful General Manager of the Transport Division of Frigoscandia, a position in which he had gained experience in the running of a large temperature-controlled fleet of both articulated and rigid vehicles. He had also worked as a manager in a cold store, learning all about pallet-racking and fork-lift trucks. Although not trained as an engineer, there was little about the technical side of the business which he did not understand, and for the finer technical points he could turn to Trevor Horton, Barrie and then Graham.

Following the MBO in 1986, the company could just about afford to replace the decrepit rigid temperature-controlled vehicles it had acquired with Maidment as they fell apart. It could not at the same time find additional money to buy tractors for the articulated fleet and so replace the owner-drivers with company

10   *Six-wheel rigid at Bridgwater.*

employees, although it retained control of what
owner-drivers bought and negotiated deals with
suppliers on their behalf. Manufacturers sometimes
lend hauliers a vehicle for a trial period and
Langdons compared what was on offer for price,
reliability and fuel consumption, before settling on
the Mercedes 4 X 2 LS as the most reliable and
economical of the tractors then available. Rather
than asking an owner-driver to find the money
for a new vehicle, the company would buy and
operate it for just over 12 months, thus being able
to claim capital allowances for tax purposes over
two years. It then sold the tractor on to an owner-
driver at a written-down price, using to the full the
facility Peter Dobbs had made available. This helped
not just the owner-drivers: it also allowed Langdons to
build up its company-owned fleet and conserve cash by avoiding tax.

11   *A Langdons' truck and
London Bridge.*

While money for capital expenditure remained tight, the company
encouraged those few owner-drivers who had consistently shown their long-
term commitment to Langdons to buy a second tractor and run the second
vehicle with a driver they employed. This privilege was extended only to those
whose accounts showed consistent cash generation. The company could have
obtained vehicles on contract hire but that would have involved making a four-

or five-year commitment and as none of Langdons' business was other than on an *ad hoc* basis, this was a risk it was not prepared to take. The one time an owner-driver took a vehicle on contract hire he contrived to write it off on a roundabout, voiding his insurance and leaving Langdons to pay for hiring a non-existent vehicle for the next two years.

In a technical sense, trailers for ambient traffic are reasonably straight-forward. You have to look out for cracks in the chassis, especially if they have been carrying a fork-lift truck attached to the back, which causes excessive flexing of the chassis and is not a good idea. With a curtain-sided trailer or flat-bed, there is not much to differentiate between manufacturers apart from cost. Refrigerated trailers pose more questions. The choice, as Langdons began to build up its temperature-controlled fleet, lay between Schmitz, two French manufacturers, and Gray and Adams from Fraserburgh in Scotland. Langdons

tested them all, finding both the French trailers inferior and poor long-term value. There then occurred a coincidence, or stroke of good fortune, which influenced future purchasing policy.

In 1990 WMAS had been involved in the MBO of the leading manufacturer of commercial fishing gear which was located in Killybegs, Co. Donegal. Expanding into the Scottish market, this company had acquired a business in Fraserburgh of which I became Chairman. As the business expanded, we moved into a factory adjacent to that occupied by

12   *Artic with driver Darren Knight.*

Gray and Adams. Naturally I got to know Jim Gray, their Chairman, and as Chairman of Langdons we shared a mutual interest in the transport industry. Jim told me that his biggest customers were the supermarkets, but their ordering patterns were such that his factory's workload throughout the year was uneven, January and February being months when few wanted deliveries – which is not surprising given the British climate.

Langdons' demand for temperature-controlled transport was not especially seasonal. With this in mind, Michael Donoghue and I suggested to Jim that we should place orders for delivery in his flat months, in return for which he gave us favourable terms. From then on Langdons used Gray and Adams both for its refrigerated trailers and for the bodies on its rigid temperature-controlled vehicles, and with up to 30 trailers being ordered in a single year this worked to the advantage of both firms.

Langdons was meticulous in drawing up the specification for its trailers. A simple, but significant, modification was the incorporation of pallet racks under the chassis, so that a driver had space to pick up empty pallets to replace those on which goods were being delivered. As we noted, a temperature-controlled trailer moves snugly up to the ramp when unloading and the store into which its pallets are discharged is unlikely to have empty pallets to replace those on which shroud-wrapped goods are being delivered. If, however, there are empty pallets available in the yard, they could be put in the external pallet racks on or off the loading bay. (Pallet carriers are, however, no longer used in fridge trailers because of excess damage.) Pallet control is an important element in running a transport business, and one we will think about later.

An important development was the incorporation in each trailer or rigid body of a moveable screen and refrigeration equipment designed so that the configuration of the vehicle could quickly be varied between chilled and sub-zero. This made it possible to use each trailer or rigid for a mixed load by allowing the driver to take one proportion of pallets of chilled and sub-zero on the outward or delivery leg, and change the ratio on the collection, or return leg. Where other firms might have to use two vehicles, Langdons used one.

Until Lloyds Bank rejected the proposal over pallet-racking at Walford Cross, Langdons did not see the need to seek other sources of finance despite offers from other lenders. After Michael Donoghue and WMAS had had to lend the £25,000 for the pallet racking, they felt the debt of loyalty they owed to Lloyds Bank through Peter Dobbs had been satisfied. Thereafter Michael normally bought tractors and trailers on hire-purchase, paying a deposit of 10 per cent and playing off one bidder against the others. He was helped in his negotiation by the strength of the company's balance sheet, which resulted from never borrowing in total more than the shareholders' equity.

The life of a trailer is much longer than five years, which is the length of a typical hire-purchase contract, but Langdons wrote trailers down heavily as soon as the hire-purchase had been paid off, thus forming a hidden asset reserve. When it was able to order tractors in batches of 10 or more, moving from Mercedes to Renault, the company negotiated a three-year guaranteed buy-back on each vehicle. This meant that the tractor remained under warranty for the whole of its working life with Langdons. When the three years expired, if it could be sold at a higher figure than the guaranteed buy-back that was an unbudgeted profit. Best of all, the buy-back meant that costs could be accurately forecast over the life of the tractor and incorporated in charges to customers.

Next to the cost of wages in a haulage company is the cost of fuel. Every day Trevor Horton brought Michael Donoghue six or seven quotations for the supply of diesel and together they planned their bunkering policy. For 10 years the outlet at the truck stop was franchised to a single supplier, but Langdons also had bunkering facilities in Bristol and then at other depots, as well as a separate facility for its own vehicles in Taunton. In the garage David Strathdee and Paul Whitehead continuously recorded the diesel consumption of each vehicle. Any excess consumption might indicate mechanical trouble although it was more likely that a driver had by-passed the tachograph, or 'wired' it in the vernacular, because he had run out of his permitted hours. There were also one or two rogue garages where less fuel might be supplied than was charged to the firm, with the driver receiving a bribe.

The workshops also recorded the usage of tyres on prime movers and trailers. As with tractors, the company ran comparative trials before settling on a single manufacturer. As the fleet grew, the tyre specialist ATS placed a fitter and supporting equipment in the garage to support the fleet, thus obviating time wasted taking the vehicles off site when needing attention.

When the company increased its palleted storage capacity, it needed more sophisticated fork-lift trucks to reach the higher layers of racking. Normally Michael Donoghue handled all major capital commitments personally, both approving the choice of supplier and monitoring the method of payment. Through an administrative error, after it had chosen the supplier of fork-lift trucks for a major expansion, the company signed a long-term contract hire agreement without referring it to Michael. With inevitable changes in the pattern of demand, many of the trucks became redundant in mid-term, but replacing them with more suitable equipment incurred high penalties. It was a costly error and one which was not repeated.

Apart from trucks, trailers and accessories, Langdons constantly needed more investment in temperature-controlled warehousing, eating up all the available space at Walford Cross, causing the garage to be relocated off the site, and eventually leading to the closure of the truck stop. All major investment decisions were subjected to board approval but, as Managing Director, Michael Donoghue never delegated the negotiation of individual contracts and kept a daily eye on the running costs of each vehicle. He could do this because of the accuracy of the data coming from the clerks in the workshops and from his accounts department. If you have up-to-date and accurate information, negotiation with traders in the private sector is straightforward. Dealing with the public sector poses new difficulties, which we will examine next.

Refrigerated trailers made by the two French manufacturers are freely available in the United Kingdom but Jim Gray told me that his had been barred from sale in France through non-tariff barriers, although the French had no qualms about the safety of Gray and Adams trailers owned by foreign firms and using their highways. WMAS was at that time involved with a firm in Leeds manufacturing dyeing machinery which had been bought out of receivership and of which I became Chairman. A dyeing machine is in essence a pressure vessel made of stainless steel. As our standard machine was some 30 per cent cheaper than its inferior French competitor, we started taking orders from French textile manufacturers. We were then told by French officials that every document, including working drawings and parts lists not seen by customers, had to be translated into French. That done, we were told that a certain grade of stainless steel must be used, which happened only to be manufactured in France. A dyeing machine needs different gauges of plate and diameters of tube. The steel manufacturer could supply some of what we wanted, but not all. We were able to buy what was unavailable to us directly from France through a third party in Sweden. We were then told that the certification of pressure vessels by Veritas or Lloyds, which are the world standards, was not acceptable in France. They would send over their own inspectors, of whom there were two. Then one of the inspectors became unavailable and the other too busy to make the journey. Deliveries came to a halt. At that stage we, and our French customers, gave up.

I was interested to know that Gray and Adams had been subjected to the same death by a thousand cuts in the 'free and unrestricted market' of which the United Kingdom was a member.

Meanwhile, we may note the following:

- Do not delegate the daily supervision of essential operating costs.
- Stop inexperienced employees entering into capital commitments.
- Identify key costs areas and set up accurate monitoring procedures.
- Test comparative products before selecting suppliers.
- Specify equipment carefully, including provision for pallet return.
- Use tax breaks to save cash.
- Where possible buy vehicles on guaranteed buy-back terms from the manufacturer.

Chapter 9
DEALING WITH PUBLIC SECTOR EMPLOYEES

There were, you may recall, two leased warehouses at Arnos Castle in Bristol, one called Arnos B used for storage of dry goods, especially paper for the Finnish company Varma, at ambient temperature, and the other, Arnos C, which was refrigerated and sub-let to Tom Granby Ltd. Both warehouses suffered from being near the centre of the city, which meant that trucks encountered traffic delays getting in and out. As the paper business diminished, Arnos B accepted other goods for storage. Because it came only in two- or three-tonne rolls, thieves left the paper alone. When, however, the store contained portable items, theft became a major problem and there can have been few public houses in Bristol one Christmas which did not see a brisk trade in mountain bikes at a heavy discount. So long as Tom Granby stayed in Arnos C, it was not a financial burden to Langdons, but with the paper stocks running down Arnos B began losing serious amounts of money.

Following the piece in the newspaper about the intentions of the Bristol Development Corporation (BDC) affecting Arnos Castle, on 18 April 1990 Rob Swindells met two of the BDC's directors who confirmed that Langdons' warehouses would almost certainly be demolished and that the work was expected to start in the summer of the following year. This information was confirmed when the development plans were published.

Michael Donoghue is meticulous about filing documents and keeping records of conversations, especially when public servants are involved. This is not because officials are dishonest or mendacious, but they operate in an environment where no individual is encouraged to accept personal responsibility, where keeping the file in order is more important than getting the work done, and where time does not cost money. After constantly pressing the BDC for information, in February 1991 Langdons received formal notice of a public enquiry concerning the compulsory purchase orders for Arnos B and C. As there were unlikely to be any objections, the BDC advised the company to make other storage arrangements, especially for Varma's paper and for Tom Granby. Tom Granby eventually found suitable premises at Avonmouth, and with effect from 1 September 1991 Langdons rented for the Varma paper the Taunton warehouse which it had occupied when Michael Donoghue joined the business but had long vacated.

13 *Walford Cross from the air in 1984 (left) and in 1998 (below).*

For those who might be interested in the detail of the subsequent negotiations, a full account is given in *Taunton Cider and Langdons*. Throughout the summer of 1991 the BDC said it could not expedite matters because it was waiting for the Secretary of State to confirm the compulsory purchase orders. When Michael Donoghue wrote to the Secretary of State early in October complaining about the delay and uncertainty, he upset the BDC who explained that it was no fault of theirs but due to 'communication problems'. It had proved fruitless pressing the land agents appointed by the BDC to agree compensation because they said they were powerless to act as they could get no instructions from their client.

On receipt of Michael Donoghue's letter, the Department of the Environment passed the buck back to the BDC and its Chairman suggested that we settle the matter across the table in Bristol without either side instructing solicitors. When Michael Donoghue and I arrived for the meeting on 17 October, we were surprised to see that the BDC's solicitor from a major London firm was present. After going through the problems we agreed that Langdons should not pay any rent on Arnos B after September 1991, and the Chairman of the BDC formally asked me, as Chairman of Langdons, to grant him '7 days' grace' without rocking the boat any more so that he could sort out the muddle.

Langdons heard nothing until 6 March 1992, when it received a peremptory demand from the BDC's agents for arrears of rent on Arnos B from the previous September, amounting to £70,125. Leaving Michael Donoghue to give the BDC his views on that suggestion, on 16 March 1992 I again wrote to the Chairman of the BDC to remind him that the seven days' grace he had asked me for had long expired.

In July 1992 the BDC paid Langdons £140,508.43 compensation for vacating Arnos B, a sum which was about what Langdons would have been prepared to give to be rid of the liabilities under the lease. The payment included substantial interest because the District Valuer, whose duties include preventing waste of public funds, was for some weeks too busy to approve it. As the BDC had failed to register for VAT, another £18,831.39 was held back while the two government bodies, the Departments of the Environment and of Customs and Excise, argued whether or not the money should be transferred from one pocket in the national coat to another.

When the time came for Langdons to agree the disturbance compensation in respect of Arnos C, there was a sense that the BDC and its long-suffering and amiable Chairman had had enough of Michael Donoghue's relentless pressure, his accurate record keeping, and his awkward Chairman. When Michael and I paid a last visit to the BDC offices to meet him and his team for a discussion about the Arnos C compensation, we took with us three boxes of files. Michael had on a previous occasion shocked the Chairman by handing him a document

14 *Walford Cross depot after closure.*

detailing every conversation members of his staff had had with Langdons. Glancing apprehensively at the boxes, the Chairman asked what figure we had in mind. We said £300,000. The Chairman said he thought £250,000 would be enough, and we split the difference. We took away the unopened boxes and some weeks later, on 11 November, received a cheque for £294,229.74, again including interest because of a delay in payment.

Our aim here is not to criticise public servants but to note how best to handle transactions in which they are involved. You must remember that each department will be protective of its corner because, if it were not, jobs might be lost. So long as the file is in order and procedures have been followed, common sense can be ignored. These people are not stupid or corrupt but they become slaves to the system and operate in a different world from that of business or commerce. The money they spend does not come from their own bank accounts. Delay, however costly, is preferable to making a decision that might be criticised. The Arnos Castle case was comparatively simple because, in essence, only one government agency, the BDC, was involved. Let us consider, for a moment, the difficulties of handling a problem where a number of public bodies are concerned.

As there is no main drainage at Walford Cross, the success of the truck stop meant that the septic tank systems constantly needed upgrading. Apart from the additional sewage generated by several hundred visitors a day, there was the effluent from the truck wash and the surface water draining from acres of roofs and concrete. The outflow ran into a small stream which was also fed from the run-off from a main highway and by the effluent from a car-breaker's yard, a garage and filling station, and some private houses. When the farmer downstream noticed that the water flowing by was sometimes less than crystal clear, his agents contacted the authorities and they contacted Langdons.

Accepting that the company had a duty to ensure that any waste water or effluent it discharged into the stream was clean, Langdons constructed a reed bed through which all its sewage and other effluent was pumped. Although the water emerging from the reed bed was pure, the environmental inspectors insisted that they had a duty to judge pollution on the fluids entering the reed bed, not leaving it, and talked darkly of their powers of closing down the business.

A main sewer lay across three of the farmer's fields the other side of the motorway which was adjacent to Langdons' site. He was happy to receive a cheque for several thousand pounds in return for granting an easement for a line of drainage pipes to be laid down his ditches. The Ministry of Transport agreed that the pipes should pass through an existing culvert under the motorway. The document authorising the laying of this pipe was to be drawn up, at Langdons' expense, by the Treasury Solicitor. Due to pressure of other legal work, this would take six months. A commercial firm of lawyers might have handled the transaction in a matter of days, but that option was not available.

While awaiting the licence to pass through the culvert, the road traffic regulations changed, raising the weight limit of vehicles to 44 tonnes. This meant that all bridges had to be inspected to see whether they could carry this load. A small culvert some 20 feet below a motorway is not much of a bridge, but it was so classified. There were so many road bridges to inspect, all more important than a culvert, that it would be a year at least before the Somerset County Council, charged with the duty of inspection, could assess the culvert. The months passed, nothing further happening until 1996. The farmer had his money and stopped complaining. The environmental inspectors kept away. No more was heard from the Treasury Solicitor's office. The culvert may eventually have been inspected. That year, however, Langdons had to close the truck stop because it needed the land for warehousing, and so the problem went away.

A third arm of the state with which a transport company in particular may become involved is the police, and here, too, Langdons' experience may be helpful to those who prefer not to attract the attention of the constabulary but would like to know how to deal with it if they do.

The hours which drivers are allowed to remain at work are strictly limited. Each vehicle has a tachometer to ensure that a record is kept of all vehicle movements. To prevent tampering with tachometers, as we noted, Langdons incurred the trouble and expense of cross-checking all vehicle fuel consumption against recorded mileage. The garage also checked tachographs to test for any interference or 'wiring'. Apart from being read mechanically in the traffic office, all used tachographs were submitted to an independent test house to ensure that drivers had made no illegal movements. On top of these precautions, the garage randomly fitted hubometers to double-check vehicle movements. Because of its reliance on owner-drivers, who might wish to bend the rules concerning rest periods, Langdons was known in the trade and by government inspectors to be rigorous about controlling driver hours. A driver who deliberately drove illegally, other than under duress, received a written warning. If it happened twice he was dismissed, even if, as in one instance, he was a personal friend of the Chairman.

In a case concerning the contravention of driving and rest regulations the prosecution does not have to show *mens rea*, or a guilty intent. The Ministry of Transport officials whose duty it is to enforce the regulations know that there are occasions when a driver cannot avoid breaking the law. The vehicle may be held up on a motorway and the driver would commit an offence whatever he did, by parking on the hard shoulder or by driving to a permitted parking area. More often a driver may be unreasonably delayed unloading and obliged to leave the ramp to park up in the nearest available place. Only moving on or off a ferry is a driver legally permitted to exceed his hours. Knowing these problems the Ministry accepts that up to one in 20 tachograph cards, each covering a day, may show a minor infringement, and that a firm with less than this amount of minor blips is doing its best to comply with the regulations.

On 9 July 1993 a driver called Woolard who had been with Langdons only three days ignored the instructions of his traffic controller, drove beyond his permitted hours and had an accident in Wiltshire. The police constable attending the scene was called Elsbury. From what Woolard told Elsbury, or what Elsbury imagined Woolard had told him, a sequence of events followed which wasted thousands of hours of police time and a drama ensued on which the curtain did not finally fall for three years. In the process a police force which, four years earlier, had been too stretched to find an officer to arrange an identity parade, was exposed as containing elements which were profligate, vindictive, gullible, incompetent and poorly led. As the details are again given in *Taunton Cider and Langdons*, an outline here will suffice.

The Wiltshire police called for Langdons' tachographs for a period of three months prior to Woolard's accident. It happened that these tachographs had already been the subject of a review by the Ministry of Transport, which had found nothing out of order. After they had been handed over, Elsbury called at Walford Cross (which is in Somerset and not Wiltshire) and indicated that he wanted to have a 'chat' with four drivers. Because he said that he did not intend to take statements, he was given a room in which to interview them without a manager or lawyer being present. At that stage, Langdons' staff trusted all police officers and wished to be helpful. They were soon to realise that life is not that simple.

On 13 October 1993 ten uniformed officers and one detective from the Wiltshire police, with one from Somerset and Avon, descended without notice on Walford Cross with a warrant signed by a magistrate empowering them to seize, among other things, all documents in the traffic office and all computer records from Rob Swindells. Until overruled by a sergeant, Elsbury refused to let the firm take copies of the seized documents, which would have brought its operations to a halt. Following the raid 12 drivers, including Woolard, who had by then left the company, received summonses relating principally to the misuse of tachographs. Eleven of the charges were dismissed with costs against the police, only Woolard being convicted.

Following this debacle, the Wiltshire Constabulary appear to have felt that it had failed in its duty to uncover some deep and fraudulent plot in which Langdons was involved. When the police approached the Ministry of Transport for its help, it refused to take part in the witch hunt. The trade press was less discreet, to the extent on one occasion of reporting a matter which had been leaked to it in breach of the Data Protection Act, and duly published articles about the impending prosecutions using information passed to it by the police. The Chief Constable of Wiltshire received a personal letter from his former boss in Somerset, advising him that he was acting foolishly in allowing his officers to harass Langdons, which he equally foolishly ignored. From my correspondence with him it became evident that he had not been told the whole truth about what his officers were doing and, despite being pointed in the right direction, was not wise enough to enquire.

Among other massive tasks, the police analysed all the drivers' pay slips to compare them with the tachograph information. Individual drivers received telephone calls from Elsbury, and perhaps others, on their mobile telephones inviting them to drop in for 'chats' at a Wiltshire police station without any lawyer present. They were reminded of the penalties they might suffer for contravening the regulations, which might be mitigated if they proved 'co-operative'. They were also asked to hand over any correspondence between themselves and the firm.

These approaches to drivers, unprofessional as they were, did no harm to the business because the drivers could do no more than tell the truth, however unpalatable it might be to the police. Langdons asked employees to do their best to achieve scheduled deliveries but not at the expense of breaking the law. More damaging commercially were the visits to Langdons' customers up and down the country by squads of Wiltshire officers, who implied that they were investigating some fraud and wished to see all relevant records of dealing with Langdons, including video footage.

The police and the Crown Prosecution Service were unable to bring any charge against Langdons because Langdons had committed no crime. Being out of time to issue fresh summonses for traffic offences, they came up with the scheme of charging 20 drivers and two traffic managers, Christopher Murt and Rupert Ryall, with conspiring to make false tachograph entries, a charge to which the six-month restriction did not apply. Two weeks before the trial they had another brilliant idea, amending the charges so that if the defendants entered a plea of not guilty they would all have to remain in court for the duration of the trial, which might last several weeks. That would have proved as damaging to the company as the denial of the right to copy documents seized by the police under their warrant.

In court the drivers pleaded guilty to technical tachograph offences. Having known that drivers sometimes had to drive off customer's premises to park up, Chris Murt and Rupert Ryall reluctantly agreed to plead guilty to aiding and abetting the tachograph offences. Having served the purpose of enabling the prosecution to proceed out of time, the conspiracy charges were dropped. The defendants were fined in total the sum of £6,750, a derisory figure in the context of normal road traffic and tachograph offences. The prosecution asked for £14,000 costs and were awarded £1,750, which was less than the amount Langdons had been awarded for the costs of the abortive first hearing.

Following the trial, the Wiltshire police opposed the renewal by the Traffic Commissioner of Langdons' operating licences. He responded by renewing them and granting 10 in addition. Undaunted, on 2 September 1998 Elsbury stopped another Langdons' lorry and, after noting a minor error, was again allowed to go on a fishing expedition outside his county boundaries to seek evidence. This time the magistrates indicated their opinion of the case, and of the Crown Prosecution Service, by imposing a fine which, with costs, amounted to less then £100.

Taunton Cider and Langdons was published in 2000. When subsequently a Langdons' lorry was involved in a fatal accident in Wiltshire, a senior officer telephoned Rob Swindells personally to apologise for the necessity by law of detaining the vehicle for inspection, assuring him that it would be returned as soon as possible. At least it seemed that policy was no longer being made at Police Constable level.

The British police labour under many disadvantages such as political interference, political correctness, an obligation to employ officers physically unsuited for the job, and society's concentration on rights rather than obligations. The constabulary would be better able to counter these influences and reassure the public if it adopted and followed through a policy of recruiting applicants of higher intelligence with leadership potential and promoted them while they were still young. The army would be equally inefficient if its leadership consisted almost entirely of middle-aged non-commissioned officers.

From these and other incidents we can learn the following lessons:

- Keep meticulous records, including notes of all conversations when dealing with official bodies.
- If an official procrastinates unduly, complain to someone higher up the chain.
- When dealing with those in authority, be patient but persistent.
- Do not let employees have unmonitored 'chats' with police officers.
- Do not rely on common sense or promptness from public servants.
- Ensure as far as possible compliance with regulations and use independent checks for tachographs.

Chapter 10

THE TAUNTON CIDER TAKE-OVER AND THE MOVE OUT OF AMBIENT TRANSPORT

One day in the summer of 1995 Michael Donoghue was travelling by air from Bristol to Edinburgh. Peter Adams, the Managing Director of Taunton Cider, was on the same flight and the two sat together on the journey. Michael had agreed with Neil Rixon, the director responsible for distribution at Taunton Cider, for Langdons to take over the warehousing at the factory in Norton Fitzwarren, as well as all the haulage. The new arrangements were due to start that autumn, in a few weeks' time. As Taunton Cider's store men and drivers would in future be working for Langdons, the two firms had retained lawyers to ensure the rights of the employees were safeguarded and that the complex employment regulations were not being infringed. Langdons had agreed to buy the Taunton Cider vehicle fleet and the price had been settled. In addition it had made further significant investment to ensure that sufficient resources would be available to handle the job in the busy run-up to Christmas. While Michael spoke enthusiastically about the future working together, Peter Adams said little. And for good reason. Taunton Cider plc was about to be taken over by Matthew Clark plc, another cider manufacturer and a distributor of intoxicants located at Shepton Mallet in East Somerset.

It made good business sense for Neil Rixon to sub-contract all his distribution functions to Langdons. The days when delivery vehicles returning to Norton Fitzwarren carried empty bottles and kegs were over, which meant that his fleet was running light for at least half its mileage. His drivers and warehouse staff belonged to a union which had a record of militancy, with strikes being called on national political or economic grounds rather than in respect of local issues. When the warehouse staff went on strike, the factory had to stop production although its staff still had to be paid. Without active union membership, Langdons had no such labour problems. It had shown its ability to handle warehousing as well as delivery on a national scale in the service it was providing for Gerber Foods. Because their trucks would be carrying return loads for other customers, by sub-contracting everything to Langdons Taunton Cider would achieve significant cost reductions.

So long as it had been owned by the major brewers with their tied houses, Taunton Cider had enjoyed a captive market. This comfortable arrangement became illegal after 1990 when the government introduced legislation to break up monopolistic and anti-competitive practices in the brewing industry. To cushion itself against the impact of the loss of guaranteed business, Taunton Cider had been able to negotiate a transitional five-year supply agreements with the brewers, but in 1995 this respite was coming to an end, and Bass, its biggest customer, was about to introduce the other major national cider manufacturer, Bulmers, into its tied public houses as a second choice for drinkers.

After the 1990 legislation, the brewers secured no special advantages by owning Taunton Cider and, with the exception of Guinness which did not own public houses, they put their shares in the company up for sale. There were three bidders: Guinness, Matthew Clark under Peter Aikens, and a management team of three directors, Peter Adams, Brian Longstaff and Andrew (or Andy) Nash. Although Guinness put in the highest bid, the other brewers were reluctant to see it take control of such an important supplier and accepted a lower offer from the MBO team of around £70 million. The MBO was duly completed on 22 May 1991. The financiers who had backed the MBO had insisted that their support was dependent on Taunton Cider Ltd becoming a publicly quoted company and this duly happened in July 1992.

As the tortuous details of these events are recounted at length in *Taunton Cider and Langdons*, there is no need to repeat them here. With the public placing of their shares, the three principal players in the MBO became rich men and included the rest of the employees in their good fortune, and many who worked in Norton Fitzwarren also saw a handsome profit on their investment. Following a family bereavement the highly respected Brian Longstaff left the firm in August 1993, handing over his duties to Neil Rixon. Peter Adams and Andy Nash remained, but in going public Taunton Cider had laid itself open to predators. Having failed to win the prize in 1991, Peter Aikens, who had once sat on Taunton Cider's board, did not intend to be denied on his second attempt.

Within three weeks of Michael Donoghue's flight to Edinburgh with Peter Adams, the news of Peter Aikens' bid on behalf of Matthew Clark became public, valuing Taunton Cider at £275 million. The employees were assured that the new owner had no intention, if the bid succeeded, of moving production from Norton Fitzwarren. With such an extravagant offer, and many shares now held by institutions, it was inevitable that on 8 November 1995 Matthew Clark plc should have become the parent company of Taunton Cider.

It was not long before the assurances about the future of Norton Fitzwarren were proved worthless. Within weeks, and shortly before Christmas, the warehouse staff were told that they would be losing their jobs because all distribution would in future be concentrated in a shared group facility, yet to be built, in Bristol. Langdons were told nothing, but the agreement Michael Donoghue had made with Neil Rixon was clearly not going to be honoured.

Having paid, as he later conceded, too much for Taunton Cider, Peter Aikens was forced to look for economies. Although its publicity made much of the cider 'coming up from Somerset where the cider apples grow', much of it was produced from imported apple pulp. The days when Kingston Blacks or Tom Tutts gave a distinctive flavour to a chemical-free product were long gone and the orchards where they had been grown are no longer a feature of the West Somerset scene. Achieving consistency of strength and taste had become the province of the chemist rather than the cider-maker.

As a glance at Mrs Beeton's masterpiece will reveal, there is nothing difficult in making cider. The trick is to persuade the public to buy your brand. That is why, in April 1991, 149 Taunton Cider employees, or exactly a third of the total staff, had been engaged in sales and other commercial activities. Cost-saving and synergy-seeking are natural consequences of takeovers. If the same product can be produced more cheaply elsewhere, then that will happen. Matthew Clark already owned Gaymers, Coates, Showerings and Whiteways, names and brands all with their following among cider and perry drinkers. There was no reason why the factory in Shepton Mallet which produced the product for them could not also, through economies of scale, make the Taunton Cider brands more cheaply than the factory at Norton Fitzwarren.

Peter Adams, perhaps wisely, decided to retire when the takeover went through. Neil Rixon and Andy Nash eventually followed. Neil's responsibility had been to see that the customers received their orders correctly and on time. Andy was a commercial director whose subsequent career confirmed both his ability and Aikens' folly in not keeping him. It did not matter where the cider was made so long as the public remained loyal to the brands and the product was available. What happened to the sales team did not directly affect Langdons. Matthew Clark's distribution policy, adopted on the advice of consultants who failed to appreciate the importance of efficient service to customers, was to change Langdons into a different company.

Instead of waiting for its central warehouse in Bristol to be built, early in 1996 Matthew Clark decided as an interim measure to use a Bristol firm called Pearsons to handle both warehousing and distribution of the cider still being made in Norton Fitzwarren. Pearsons had no experience of the drinks trade. Neil Rixon, who had not been consulted when these decisions were made, found himself asked to maintain supplies to supermarkets and other customers from a warehouse 50 miles from the factory, using store men strange to the product. Operating from a difficult and inaccessible site, with a scheduler and clerks unfamiliar with the business, he had to give preference to a haulier with no experience in the trade.

As the disaster unfolded Langdons offered to help Pearsons by lending them free of charge a scheduler and clerk who were familiar with the Taunton Cider business, so that at least the trailers would be loaded with the right product at the right time with the right paperwork. Pearsons said no. Because everything was usually running late, rather than waste drivers' time Langdons incurred the expense of leaving trailers on the site to facilitate loading without detaining tractors. Invariably these were the last to be loaded, if at all. The more profitable deliveries were kept for Pearsons' own vehicles or given to Matthew Clark's normal haulier,

BOC Baker, with Langdons being allocated whatever these firms did not want or could not handle. Langdons' vehicles often had to return to Taunton laden with product rejected by the customer because it had been wrongly picked or delivered too late, and Langdons had to store the rejects indefinitely because nobody at Matthew Clark was detailed to sort out the problems.

As if the folly of destroying an efficient supply chain were not enough, Matthew Clark decided simultaneously to introduce the OPUS information technology (IT) programme to replace the two systems Taunton Cider had been using, which were the SAP R3 protocol and another IT package which was imperfect but just functional if managed by those familiar with it. Seeking in its later statements to explain the dramatic fall in Taunton Cider's turnover, Matthew Clark spoke of cheap cider imports and alcopops. The truth was simpler. The wounds came not from outside, but were self-inflicted, in part by accepting the advice of consultants who had failed to appreciate that efficient delivery to the customer is as important a function as manufacture.

Langdons' business with Taunton Cider continued to diminish throughout 1996. So long as production continued at Norton Fitzwarren, the cider had to be ferried to Bristol. Initially Langdons' drivers had access to Pearsons' warehouse to check their loads and could, at least, ensure their deliveries were free of error and the paperwork was in order. When, however, Pearsons turned it into a bonded warehouse and excluded Langdons' drivers, the problems became acute, incorrectly picked loads being accompanied by inaccurate documentation. It did not take long for the mistakes and failures to upset Taunton Cider customers, and especially the supermarkets, which in turn led to the significant drop in sales.

15   *The former cider factory at Norton Fitzwarren.*

By January 1997 it was obvious that the business relationship between Langdons and Matthew Clark was coming to a close. In February Matthew Clark stopped paying Langdons' invoices and it was June, after the issue of a writ, before the bills were finally settled in full with interest and costs. Before that, on 25 March, Langdons sold by auction its remaining ambient trailers and surplus tractors, so that in future the company would only be concerned with temperature-controlled storage and distribution.

We have already drawn attention to what may seem to be obvious, the importance of load factors in a transport business. The first priority is to ensure that outward vehicles are fully loaded, which means that a firm needs regular business from local suppliers. Taunton Cider was the key customer for Langdons' ambient business. Wansborough in Watchet was useful with its deliveries of paper, but Watchet is away on the North Somerset coast and Wansborough had a sister transport company, Griggs, which took the bulk of the business. Pritex, the foam subsidiary of Relyon in Wellington, was important but, because Langdons' trailers were not high enough to carry optimum light loads, never more than marginally profitable. SmithKlineBeecham, with its drinks from Coleford, was too far away, and Lafarge, with its plasterboard, involved a 50-mile journey to Avonmouth before picking up a load. The Varma paper had virtually disappeared, as had the ICI nitrates. All these customers had been valuable but had become peripheral. Without Taunton Cider the heart was torn out of Langdons' ambient business. Fortunately, as we will see, there were more exciting opportunities opening up in temperature-controlled operations.

The takeover of Taunton Cider by Matthew Clark is a case study in what not to do. Of all the mistakes made by Peter Aikens and his consultants, overlooking the importance of warehousing and distribution was possibly the greatest. Simultaneously to change hauliers, warehouses and IT systems was the height of folly. By April 1998 the combined businesses of Matthew Clark had declined to the extent that its net assets had fallen to £95.4 million. It was then taken over by an American company called Canandaigua Ltd. The Norton Fitzwarren employees had lost their jobs and the land on which the factory stood is being redeveloped for housing.

- Always run a new IT system in parallel with the old one until it has been proved effective.
- Do not incur major costs for a new contract until it has been signed.
- Do not let consultants take management decisions.
- It is better to win market share from a competitor than to buy the competitor out.
- If part of your business stops being viable, shut it down.
- Manufacture, distribution and consumption are three legs of the same stool.

Chapter 11

SETTING UP THE TEMPERATURE-CONTROLLED SHARED-USER OPERATION CALLED CHILLNET

Hauling a full trailer-load of goods from one point to another at ambient temperature is not a complex operation. Large national firms negotiate long-term contracts with manufacturers and supermarkets which guarantee them a base business. These arrangements may include intermediate warehousing with the additional revenue that comes from storage, picking and cross-docking. To offer a national service they need strategically placed depots and warehouses, something smaller firms do not have.

At the other end of the scale are the operators with few vehicles and low overheads, competing for chance loads on an *ad hoc* basis and obtaining some regular local business. These firms also work as sub-contractors (or 'subbies') for larger companies which need them from time to time to supplement their capacity. It is not expensive to buy or hire tractors and trailers which have seen their best years elsewhere, or to obtain an Operator's Licence. Competition from the small firms ensures that merely 'selling wheels', or simply providing transport, is low-margin work. Because of these factors, in its ambient business Langdons had always been squeezed between the national operators with modern warehouse facilities and the low-cost private firms. Without the Taunton Cider business the future looked grim.

The cost of entering the temperature-controlled distribution market is greater than for the ambient. The articulated tractors are the same but the trailers or refrigerated bodies for rigids are much more expensive. In addition, the haulier may have to provide evidence that the load has been kept at the required temperature while in its custody, and to do that it needs an efficient back-office organisation.

Once Langdons had secured the Gerber business and built its refrigerated store, it could afford to concentrate solely on temperature-controlled business. As we noted, most of the Gerber pallets went to the RDCs of the supermarkets, and the spare capacity on the trailers, which were seldom fully loaded with Gerber product, was available to carry other firms' pallets to the same destinations or to their locality. In addition to finding customers to provide this extra business on the outward leg, it was just as important to secure refrigerated loads back to the west country.

50

Langdons had one piece of unexpected good fortune. A few years previously a quoted company had set up a chilled distribution service not dissimilar to the Palletways model, and to cover the south-west it had offered to buy Langdons. Michael Donoghue and I had even got as far as the palatial offices of its merchant bank in London before accepting a cup of coffee there, chatting for a few minutes, and walking away. It had then bought a company showing high profits from its business with a single customer but which relied on contract hire for its equipment. The purchase price, calculated on a multiple of past profit rather than the value of assets, was excessive and included a huge amount of 'goodwill'. The lucrative contract was soon lost, the goodwill had to be written off, and the parent company ran into trouble, leaving many of its customers looking for someone more reliable to handle their chilled and frozen distribution.

Rob Swindells, after handing over his duties as Operations Manager to Chris Murt, had not needed any other staff to assist him in the commercial and selling function which he performed first from his office at Arnos Castle, and then from Walford Cross. Until 1995 Langdons had comparatively few customers, most of them substantial businesses whose traffic managers dealt with Rob himself or with Michael Donoghue. Everything changed when the ambient work came to an end. Chris Murt was able to amalgamate the two traffic desks, promoting one of Rupert Ryall's assistant traffic managers, the youthful Arran Osman, which gave him more time to supervise the chilled warehouse and retrain the staff for their new duties in assembling loads daily to customers' orders. The reorganisation also released Rupert to work with Rob Swindells in looking for new temperature-controlled customers.

In 1996 Langdons had only two refrigerated rigid lorries for local collection and delivery, and it was obliged at first to hire others, which Michael Donoghue did on a 'spot' or short-term basis rather than taking on the cheaper but more dangerous commitment of contract hire. Although most of the new customers were looking for chilled delivery, to provide a complete service Langdons had also to offer a sub-zero facility. As sub-zero loads for consolidation had also to be cross-docked before being sorted and sent to another hub, this meant building a sub-zero store at Walford Cross. Langdons remained short of sub-zero storage capacity until a third major extension at Walford Cross was built in September 1999. Before then, the obsolete 18-pallet trailers, which it was uneconomical to put on the road except in an emergency, often had to be used as extra static storage.

Langdons had enjoyed a good relationship with its tenant at Arnos Castle, Tom Granby, and with its Manager Director, Michael Redmond, both in business and on a personal basis. When Michael first tried to buy Tom Granby from its German owners, he had asked me to meet him at their office south of Dublin to help with the negotiation. My recollection is that the encounter was not dissimilar to my experience with TKM's Disposals Manager. Michael Redmond's bosses were not happy with this intruder who told them their proposals were ill thought out and that they would get nowhere by pressing him to pay excessively for a business which, over-burdened with debt, would

16   ChillNet advertisement.

probably founder, leaving the vendors to pick up the pieces. We reached no conclusion on that occasion but I was delighted to learn that Michael was able next time round to buy Tom Granby on more favourable terms.

Tom Granby's move from Arnos Castle to the TDG warehouse in Avonmouth had not worked out well. Because the depot was losing money, Michael Redmond offered to hand over his entire south-western storage and distribution business to Langdons, who were already doing most of the trunking between his depots. To facilitate the transfer, two of his Bristol-based managers, Cliff Carless and Brian Barrington, agreed to join Langdons, bringing with them knowledge of the Tom Granby business and consolidation skills with which Langdons' staff were less familiar.

In addition to its main operation at Knowsley near Liverpool, Tom Granby rented an office and store from TDG at Luton, from which it handled its business in the south-east. In Scotland it used a firm based at Darnley near Glasgow called Scotfrost. Seeing that, between them, Tom Granby and Langdons already possessed the skeleton of a national network, Michael Redmond, Rob Swindells and Rupert Ryall, with the enthusiastic support of everyone else involved, developed the plan to set up an organisation which would offer for chilled and frozen pallets the same kind of service that had been developed for ambient pallets by Palletways, but based on regional hubs rather than one which was central. They would publish a standard tariff based on the number of pallets and the distance involved, and expect to achieve next day delivery to all but the remoter parts of the United Kingdom. Searching for a name, Michael came up with 'Foodline'. Rob then proposed 'ChillNet' and that is the name the observant motorist now sees on the roundels on the back of vehicles up and down the land.

Three bases, or hubs, in England were clearly insufficient to service the entire country efficiently. Under the plan, goods had to be trunked overnight between hubs, each articulated lorry (artic) making a round trip when the traffic is lighter. The rigids, or smaller non-articulated lorries, would then undertake the local delivery of the pallets, collecting outward traffic to take back to the hub as they did so. The plan would only work to optimum efficiency if both the artics and the rigids could do their trips within the hours allowed to one driver. The rigids had also to return to the hub in time for their loads to be cross-docked, sorted and then reloaded for transfer to the appropriate hub elsewhere.

The potential customers for ChillNet were spread throughout the country. The initial absence of hubs in the Midlands and the north of England required some of the rigids to travel excessive distances and made the overnight trunking less efficient. For a short time in 1996 a firm based in Alcester joined the consortium and provided a hub for the Midlands. It had been a condition of its joining ChillNet that it would expand its chilled storage facilities into sub-zero and acquire enough rigids to supplement its fleet of artics, but when Michael Donoghue and I visited them to talk about their timetable for these developments it became clear their finances would not allow them to make the necessary investment. The Midlands gap was only closed after Langdons had opened its own depot in Redditch. The north ceased to be problem when David Price Food Services from Wallsend joined the consortium in 2001.

We will look later at the part that information technology played in the rapid expansion and success of ChillNet. Equally important was the personal traffic experience of Rob Swindells and Rupert Ryall, who were the first contact of any customer with an enquiry or a complaint. Both men had driven heavy goods vehicles and knew the business from bottom to top. If a customer wanted a quotation, he received it there and then. If his pallets were late or damaged, he was not put through to a clerk but spoke to someone who knew the problem and how it might be solved. Watching them in their office, an observer would think they did very little selling and a great deal of trouble-shooting but, not wishing to denigrate their marketing skills, before long ChillNet began selling itself, and this owed much to the drivers, the warehouse staff and everyone else involved in the operation. They were providing, within two years, a service which the supermarket operator Tesco, in an unpublished internal review, rated as the most efficient in the country.

While a small producer of chilled or frozen foods had previously been able in theory to sell direct to a supermarket or another customer situated at a distance, without a fixed national tariff available it had been difficult in practice to work out the price of transport. There was also the problem of seeking to achieve for customers next-day delivery every day of the year apart from Christmas Day and Easter Sunday. The only sure way these producers had been able to supply the national market was through merchants or co-operatives who had access to delivery slots at RDCs and were making consolidated deliveries. Naturally the cost of the middleman had to be met by the producer, significantly reducing his income. The service offered by ChillNet, therefore, was a boon to the smaller producers of dairy products and chilled foods, which have to get to the market regularly within a tight time limit but seldom need to send more than a few pallets. The fact that their customers knew that they could rely on anything they ordered being delivered at the right temperature and on time also helped their marketing.

Small producers without temperature-controlled storage capacity are also able to produce in more economical batches by using ChillNet because it allows them to hold in a Langdons' hub stocks of both sub-zero and chilled food to be called off as required. As the pallets will be cross-docked into and out of a ChillNet store in any event, the extra charge for holding them until called off is minimal.

With the business growing rapidly in England, Scotland and Wales, Rob Swindells was anxious to develop the Irish market with its numerous producers of dairy and meat products, most of whom had no direct access to English and continental customers. Through a relationship with Procter and Gamble, Langdons were already dealing with a firm called Shannon Transport in Limerick. Because WMAS was involved in a telecommunication company in Shannon, of which I was Chairman, I had to go there every month or so and it was no trouble for me to call in on Shannon Transport. My experience in Limerick was typical of similar visits to potential customers around the world. At first you cannot get through the door, but if you are persistent and have a product which they need you will eventually succeed. And so it was with

Shannon Transport, which joined the consortium in August 1999 with Michael O'Riordon and Dennis Hoctor becoming valuable members of the team.

One of the more difficult aspects of managing a transport business is dealing with claims from customers, and this is something we will be looking at shortly. The problem at ChillNet was exacerbated by the division of responsibility where hubs are being operated by different companies. The situation at Luton was even more trying, with TDG running the warehouse, Tom Granby managing the traffic, and Langdons doing much of the trunking and the south-western collection and delivery. Tom Granby was by then ill equipped to operate a transport fleet, even after it had concentrated on rigids rather than artics. Because it used contract hire for its vehicles, its transport costs were excessive, and the situation was made even more difficult by the shortage of drivers in the south-east, so that those employed by Tom Granby had to be supplemented by others supplied by agencies. Agency drivers are not just more expensive, they are perforce less familiar with customer location and access.

Having bought Tom Granby, Michael Redmond could not afford the investment needed to replace his rigids by company-owned vehicles. He was not making any money out of transport and there were constant arguments about whose fault it had been when a claim for late or wrong delivery came from a customer. Although the difficulty over allocating blame never went away entirely, it was at least eased when, on 1 December 1999, Langdons took over all of Tom Granby's transport operations, including its drivers and the liability for the contract hire of some fifty rigids. It was a price worth paying to bring all the transport operations under the efficient management of Chris Murt and Arran Osman, with the maintenance being done more efficiently and at lower cost by Graham Millard, Trevor Horton and their in-house team.

ChillNet would not have succeeded, for all the contribution of the management, the drivers and warehouse staff, without efficient control over three other elements of the business, namely credit control, pallet control and the settlement of claims. These are areas which deserve our attention next. Meanwhile we can note the following:

- When buying another business, give greater weight to underlying assets than to past profit.
- Depute senior employees to deal directly with customer enquiries and complaints.
- Target your investment towards the most pressing capital requirement.
- If you have a good product, persist in explaining it to the potential customer.
- If you cannot afford to do all the business yourself, use associates who are honourable and likeable.
- Remember that a unique selling proposition is unlikely to remain unique.

Chapter 12

CREDIT, CLAIMS AND PALLETS

There is nothing so painful in business as a bad debt. You incur a loss and you lose a customer. Worst of all, it damages your cash flow and, as we all know, cash is king. In the transport and distribution industry there are virtually no cash transactions and customers habitually owe their haulier money. The usual terms provide for payment within 30 days, but as statements are normally sent at the end of the month even good payers take on average 45 days' credit. A large regular customer may operate a 'self-billing' system, raising its own invoices, and this needs careful watching because its records may well not be as accurate as yours and the errors seldom work in favour of the supplier.

When Langdons served fewer, but larger, customers in the ambient business, it could obtain a copy of their latest filed accounts and assess their creditworthiness. Relying on references is less helpful, as referees tend to be guarded in their response. Because of potential exposure to possible bad debt, Langdons is cautious about taking on any new major customer. If Rob Swindells, as a good salesman, has always been anxious to clinch an order, the more cautious Michael Donoghue would want to know why the business was available. A call to the prospect's current contractor might reveal a history of an excess of claims or a bad payment record, and that the customer was one it would be happy to lose. If the business is already being handled by a competitor, it is prudent to tell them its customer is restless. Within the industry the larger firms regularly use each other's services, and keeping the reciprocal trade is more important than poaching business. Predators in any environment tend to be unloved.

Decisions about taking on major new customers were not always easy, nor did the team get them all right. When the Varma contract for storing and hauling newsprint was running down, a printing company associated with Robert Maxwell asked Langdons to tender for all its business. The geographical spread was ideal, the volume heavy for both transport and storage, and the price attractive. Anyone publicly throwing doubt on Maxwell's probity at the time might expect a writ for defamation, which had not stopped rumours about his financial affairs circulating. Michael Donoghue agreed to accept the work provided the firm provided a bank guarantee to cover its indebtedness. As bank guarantees are almost impossible to obtain within the United Kingdom without depositing the cash in escrow, the business went elsewhere. Langdons was not always so far-sighted. It accepted regular work from another manufacturer of paper products despite the somewhat unprepossessing demeanour of its proprietor, who in due course 'did a Phoenix', setting up a new business and leaving the suppliers of his old company, including Langdons, unpaid.

With the rapid expansion of the customer base after the introduction of ChillNet, Christine Lock became the first line of credit control, and as the business grew she was joined by Mary Climo. The system evolved so that each new customer was assessed, given a credit rating, and informed of the credit limit. On the rare occasions when a job was accepted from someone who had not opened an account, payment had to be made by credit or debit card. If an account became two weeks overdue, the customer received a warning that it would go on 'stop', or not be serviced until the debt had been paid. If it remained unpaid for a further week, Langdons suspended delivery of any goods in its custody and took legal action to recover the debt.

Many failures come suddenly and unexpectedly. The haulier is one of the suppliers a struggling business can least afford to lose and is likely to receive normal payment until the cash has run out. Without entering into legal niceties about general and other liens, when a customer goes into administration or receivership the only chance there is of recovering part of the loss is to refuse to hand over goods in store or in transit. In most cases, frozen foods retain their value, although on one occasion nobody wanted 40 pallets of sub-zero shelled coconuts, and it cost Langdons £2,500 to dump them. Another time it was equally expensive to dispose of tonnes of dates which proved unpalatable even to the monkeys in Bristol Zoo. Chilled goods with short sell-by dates are less of a lever for extracting cash than frozen and usually involve cutting a deal with a receiver or administrator within hours of his appointment.

Where there is heavy mutual trading between Langdons and companies like Tom Granby and TDG, it is important to establish written set-off agreements, although even then there may be legal disputation. Without such evidence, if either company failed its receiver could demand full payment from the other, which in turn would be an unsecured creditor of its former trading partner and would probably receive nothing of what it was owed.

Christine Lock and Mary Climo's tact and skill mean that Langdons have to reserve no more than 0.05 per cent of its turnover for bad debts. Their task as credit controllers is complicated by deductions customers make from their payments in respect of claims, some valid, many spurious, but all requiring management time and effort to resolve. Until he reached retirement age in 1996 Glan Robottom dealt with these claims, along with other insurance and administrative issues. The poisoned chalice has now been handed down to the current Commercial Director, Pat Griffiths. (Like other Langdon veterans, Glan still had a contribution to make and stayed with the firm on a part-time basis in another capacity for a further six years.)

Langdons accepts business on the basis of the Road Haulage Association's Conditions of Carriage 1998. Each new customer has formal notice of these

Conditions. Every two years all customers receive by recorded delivery a reminder of the contract terms, with a request to acknowledge receipt, which only seven out of ten do. The Conditions of Carriage exempt the haulier from any damages arising from late delivery or from any consequential loss. Because the haulier's liability of £1,300 per tonne is inadequate to cover the value of chilled or frozen foods, Langdons increase it to £3,000 per tonne and advise the customer that it should consider taking out additional cover if £3,000 seems insufficient.

The simplest claims to settle are those which relate to damage in transport. There is little margin of error for a fork-lift driver in a store with high racking, or loading a trailer with inches to spare for the pallet which may be carrying overhanging cases. Claims based on deterioration of the product through not being kept at the correct temperature can be more difficult to handle, not because of a lack of evidence but because they are often bogus. For example, the recipient of the goods who has over-ordered and does not want the delivery may tell the driver to open the temperature-controlled compartment and then let it warm up for half an hour without unloading it, before testing the temperature and rejecting the consignment. To counter this practice, which regrettably has been used by the most blue-chip of companies, Langdons records by satellite-tracking not just the time of arrival at the RDC loading ramp but the time when the compartment door is opened and the temperature when it is

opened. With a complete record of the temperature of every pallet in every environment in which the goods have been stored or carried since Langdons took responsibility for it, the only temperature-based claims which may be valid are those when the refrigeration plant on the vehicle is faulty or the driver has made an incorrect setting.

Other claims may relate to wrong or short deliveries. An order may, very rarely, have been incorrectly picked. With stretch-wrapping, shortages due to theft should be eliminated, although it does not always stop a dishonest storeman at an intermediate stop taking a case or two from the top of a stretch-wrapped but non-shrouded pallet which is due to be delivered to another customer. If that happens

18 *A reach truck at Bridgwater.*

more than once, the driver needs to check his remaining pallets when he visits that store before moving on.

For every delivery, the driver should receive a signed Proof of Delivery (POD) from the recipient. Unless there is a POD, the customer, or its IT system, may claim that it did not receive the goods and refuse to pay, which in turn means that the supplier satisfies a claim against the haulier by deducting it from what he owes. With honourable firms, Langdons is able to prove by satellite-tracking records when and where the vehicle made the delivery, but not all firms are able to resist the temptation to avoid paying if they can help it. As a back-up to the POD, drivers ask the recipient to sign, print their name, and write the date on the manifest relating to the delivery. Even then there are rogues who try to avoid payment, mainly in the meat trade, and they, soon detected, are best avoided.

Supermarkets, as we might expect, make their own rules. Some operate a 'drop and drive' routine, where tomorrow's driver picks up today's PODs. Tesco issue their own PODs, on a piece of paper the size of a playing card. If the customer cannot produce it the account may not be paid, and once again the haulier picks up the tab.

There are, as you would expect with such a complicated business once temperature-control is added to other factors, many ways in which things can go wrong, and the blame is always placed on the haulier because it is simpler to deduct money from a debt than to claim damages from someone else. After, for example, Langdons had sent a pallet for St Lucia to Yorkshire, and vice versa, there were no arguments. When, however, a Plymouth customer wrongly labelled two consignments of butter so that the Prague delivery went to a supermarket in the United Kingdom and the supermarket delivery to Prague, it would not have mattered if the butter had been marked with the same sell-by date. Sell-by dates are marketing tools as much as health warnings. The UK dates were much shorter than those for Prague. The supermarket rejected the butter because the dates were too long. Prague rejected it, too, because the dates were too short. Both refused to pay the supplier, who then debited Langdons. You either allow the claim, or tell the customer to pay up and probably lose the business. Langdons allowed the claim and went to collect the butter. Surprise, surprise – in neither destination was it available.

The biggest claims arise when an entire load is stolen. Over the years, and at least once with connivance from a dishonest employee, trailers have been hauled away and last seen somewhere such as on the ferry from Brindisi to Greece. That particular class of theft became less easy with the introduction of satellite-tracking, and the canny thief these days takes the vehicle or trailer to a secluded spot nearby and waits to see if somebody comes to collect it. If the police were interested in theft, they could set a trap to catch the villains. Letting them impound a trailer on which the palleted goods have a short sell-by date is not a wise move and, as we discovered with the Wiltshire Constabulary, they determine their own priorities, with robbery seldom at the top of the list. It is simpler just to go and collect the vehicle.

The third unglamorous feature which needs constant vigilance in the transport business is pallet control. 'White' pallets come in various qualities and sizes other than the standard 1,200 x 1,000 mm and, as a rule, when a delivery is made on white pallets, the haulier picks up an equal number of empty pallets. If shortages occur it is not too expensive to find or buy replacements. Many firms find it cheaper to write off white pallets than to collect them, especially when they are using a third-party haulier to make the delivery and will be charged for the return journey. Langdons are fortunate that another firm at Honiton in which WMAS is interested has just such a supplier and provides a regular source of free white pallets.

'Blue' pallets, or those owned by Chep and hired throughout industry, are a different matter. There are a variety of different contractual arrangements between Chep and its customers into which, fortunately, we do not need to probe deeply. Suffice it to say that a haulier must ensure that his drivers and other staff account with customers for blue pallets in such a way that there any claims for shortages can be rebutted, or the missing pallets replaced from elsewhere. If Langdons had to replace all the 24 Chep pallets used on a single delivery, it would cost over £300, or more than the job was worth. Thanks to the skill first of the young Pat Griffiths and now of Chris Camp and his team, that doesn't happen. Pallet control is a tedious, repetitive task requiring constant attention to detail in what can be a somewhat murky environment, but a haulier neglects it at his peril.

Let us note the following points:

- Do not give credit to anyone you do not trust.
- Enforce credit control strictly.
- Ensure that all customers have formal notice of your conditions of trade.
- Use satellite-tracking on all vehicles.
- Keep records of temperature at every stage while handling chilled or frozen goods.
- Deal promptly and in detail with claims.
- Tell a customer who makes bogus claims to find another contractor.
- Give due attention to pallet control.

Chapter 13

REFINANCING AND SUNNY DELIGHT

As we saw, Langdons installed refrigeration into the existing store at Walford Cross and paid for it with the windfall it received when the warehouses at Arnos Castle were bought through a Compulsory Purchase Order. Having entered the temperature-controlled storage business, there never seemed to be enough pallet spaces to service the work which was available and during this period the builders were seldom absent from Walford Cross as sections of the old building were successively converted to this new use. Before long the vehicle workshop had to be moved off the site because it was taking up valuable space, even though that involved the prime movers and trailers running eight unnecessary miles each time they needed servicing.

Building or converting cold stores is a specialist business. For its construction work, Langdons used as architect the talented Kenneth Steel, who combined elegant design with practicality and economy. The technical aspect was handled by Wilf Dickinson, whose experience in cold store construction is unequalled. Kenneth and Wilf were to work together as a team for the next decade on the various extensions and new-build projects both at Walford Cross and in Bridgwater, bringing in all their completions on time and within budget. A cold store is not simply a large insulated box. The floor, especially for a sub-zero operation, has to remain stable despite an environment of minus 25 degrees Centigrade on one side and the heat sink of the soil on the other. Apart from the specification and installation of the refrigeration plant, there are numerous other matters to take into consideration, such as sprinklers, the number and location of the loading bays, facilities for the charging of fork-lift trucks, office and rest accommodation for the staff, and the installation of the high pallet racking.

The architect and his engineering colleague must also pay special attention to fire risks. Flammable material may be used for insulation and firemen cannot enter a cold store to deal with a conflagration because they might have to work under burning plastic, or what the soldiers call napalm. Where a wall of the store is within a certain distance of other buildings, the insulation has to be of more expensive fire-resistant material. You cannot obtain insurance cover for the building or its contents without a Fire Certificate, which is granted after a visit from an officer in the Fire Service. As with all such inspections, the official has to justify his presence and importance by finding something wrong. On one extension at Walford Cross, he insisted on changes to a wall involving a wasted expenditure of £16,000. The ruling was not in line with the fire regulations but an appeal could take up to 18 months, during which there would be no Fire Certificate, no insurance, and no cold store. From then on, Wilf introduced a simple error into any building needing a Fire Certificate, such as an extractor fan in a fire wall, which the Fire Officer would then portentously discover and go away happy, leaving a cost of under £200 for rectification and compliance.

Refrigeration plants use a lot of electricity. Apart from the sub-station at Walford Cross, Wilf had to install a generator which could kick in whenever the mains supply failed. My house being on the same electrical loop as the store, I often stole up quietly when our lights went out to ensure that the generator was working, the palleted goods were not defrosting and, equally important, that our IT systems had not gone down. There are, however, circumstances for which no provision can be made, as when Stan, the yard shunter (I'll omit his surname to avoid any embarrassment), having parked on a gentle slope, went to check that a trailer's brakes were off without making sure that those of the tractor were on. The rig rolled forward, only coming to a halt when it had demolished a pylon carrying the electricity supply for half of Taunton. Fortunately, we had a stand-by generator. They did not.

In the spring of 1997 the American conglomerate Procter and Gamble carried out a test marketing project in Cumbria with their chilled fruit-based drink called 'Sunny Delight'. Encouraged by the result, the German managers responsible for its introduction into Europe gave a contract to Gerber in Bridgwater to produce the drink. They planned to launch it throughout the United Kingdom in the summer of 1998. As Gerber had no facility for storage and picking, it referred the men from Hamburg to Langdons.

Procter and Gamble said that, apart from the special launch arrangements, they would need permanent chilled storage capacity for 5,000 pallets. Langdons would also have to deliver up to 70 loads a day. Still smarting from the Taunton Cider debacle, Michael Donoghue agreed to provide the necessary facilities provided Procter and Gamble entered into a firm contract appointing Langdons as the sole contractor for at least five years. This they agreed, and the details, including the rates, were then thrashed out and confirmed in writing. All these arrangements were made by the Germans without informing their British colleagues in Newcastle, and by-passing in particular the manager responsible for Procter and Gamble's transport in the United Kingdom and Ireland. He had never met Langdons and understandably was less than pleased about having this unknown haulage firm thrust upon him. Unable to take it out on his continental colleagues, he found an easier target closer to home. Nor was he mollified when, in 2000, Langdons were rated by Procter and Gamble as their most reliable haulier in Great Britain, with no deliveries missed out of seventy thousand.

Finding the vehicles to carry out the distribution would not be a problem as surplus loads can be sub-contracted. The difficulty was with the storage space as there was no spare capacity at Walford Cross and the warehouse staff were already struggling to keep pace with the current volume. To meet its commitment for Sunny Delight the firm would have to construct another large store, taking up the remaining suitable space in the yard, including that occupied by the truck stop. Michael Donoghue and his colleagues had decided long ago that Langdons was a distribution company rather than a caterer. The decision to give up the truck stop was painful, but not difficult. Finding the £1.5 million to provide the extra facilities was something else.

Watching the business grow, a number of investors and local businessmen and women had indicated they would like to take a stake in the company if that became a possibility. Some of these people had previously invested in other companies with which WMAS had been associated. Others, such as Wilf Dickinson, knew the business or were friends of individual directors. The original partners were delighted when Chris Murt and Rupert Ryall, the two employees who had been disgracefully treated by the Wiltshire police and the Crown Prosecution Service, also asked if they could become shareholders. To ensure that they retained control of policy, the directors decided they did not want any third party taking up too large a share, other perhaps than the quoted investment company which had, in a previous venture with WMAS, shown exemplary conduct by giving advice when asked without ever interfering.

You will recall how Michael Donoghue, Rob Swindells and Paul Rowe had formed a management company which, with the support of Peter Dobbs at Lloyds Bank, had paid out the original outside investors in 1987. By buying that company Langdons was able effectively to acquire its own shares without going to the court for approval. As Langdons' net asset value, aided by a revaluation of the freehold site at Walford Cross, had increased by a factor in excess of ten times in the decade since the MBO, the directors were able to issue nine new shares for every old one, and then offer them for sale at £2 each. With 75,000 old shares available, this meant there were 750,000 new ones and, at £2 each, this produced the required £1.5 million. It also meant that every pound introduced by Michael, Rob and Paul, by re-mortgaging their homes and borrowing from their families at the time of the MBO, was now an asset valued at £20.

Most companies find that raising money from new issues is an expensive and time-consuming business. That was not the case here. The directors asked the auditors to undertake the process known as due diligence to provide reassurance to the new shareholders, although none of them requested this. In addition to the auditors' costs, stamp duty had to be paid on the new share issue and registration fees. But that was all. The total cost of the issue amounted to less than £15,000. The outside shareholders were given further safeguards: together they were allotted 28 per cent of the equity, which meant that, with less than 75 per cent remaining in their hands, the four original partners could not combine to change the Articles of Association or ride roughshod over the other members; and two experienced financier investors, William Underwood and

Clockwise from top left: Arran Osman, Spencer Dixon, Rob Swindells, Paul Rowe.

Clockwise from top left: Patrick Griffiths, Chris Davies, David Every-Clayton, Rupert Ryall.

John Rix, joined them on the board. William and John proved both critical and supportive, which was their correct function, and remained with the company until it was sold in 2004.

The local office of a firm of stockbrokers had suggested that some of their private clients might like to buy shares. After the allocations had been made, they offered to find other investors if any shareholder wanted to sell or, in effect, to make an informal market in Langdons' shares. This was an attractive idea, as it might have led to the gradual transition from a private to a publicly quoted company, had that route been chosen. Unfortunately, or perhaps fortunately, nobody ever wanted to sell and it was left to the board to tell the investment company which held shares what they thought they were worth each year.

Procter and Gamble introduced Sunny Delight to the national market in March 1998. Prior to the launch, to ensure the expected demand could be met, Chris Murt had the task of finding chilled storage spaces for 20,000 pallets. Of these, 6,000 were located at a TDG store in Willand, just over the Devon border, a facility which was still needed after the completion of the new 5,000-pallet store at Walford Cross. Chris also located another five cold stores to hold stock temporarily. The launch was backed by massive advertising. Newspapers published articles about this amazing new soft drink which had taken the market by storm and its competitors by surprise. The demand was huge. In the sixth week Langdons delivered 10,600 pallets, a figure never again to be achieved. With the Bridgwater factory under pressure, Procter and Gamble financed a new plant and warehouse which opened in Blackburn in April 1999. Here Gerber produced Sunny Delight and Langdons managed the warehouse and the distribution, with Paul Street, an experienced Langdons traffic controller, moving north to take charge.

In the wake of its success in the United Kingdom, Procter and Gamble launched Sunny Delight in Ireland. Here the miffed Newcastle staff took control, handing the business to Shannon Transport in Limerick, as we previously noted. Procter and Gamble also started producing the drink near Barcelona to supply the French, Portuguese and Spanish markets, and asked Langdons to set up a transport subsidiary there to handle the distribution and to open a depot in Holland. These were kind and generous proposals which, after a thorough investigation of both, in England, by Michael Donoghue and a more superficial one by me in Spain, the board rejected. It limited its involvement to sending artics to work out of Barcelona for a few months and continued to supply northern Europe from England.

Those months in early 1998 proved very hectic for Langdons. Within two short years of losing Taunton Cider, the firm had recreated itself in a new and more profitable form. It was well financed and had a strengthened board of directors. Despite the damaged *amour propre* in Newcastle, the Procter and Gamble contract had five years to run at good rates. What could go wrong? A great deal, as it happened.

The re-introduction of outside shareholders to Langdons in 1997 marked the end of the recovery phase. The multiple of 20 on the original investment by the three managers, or 14 times by WMAS, was greater than is usual when a loss-making business has been acquired by MBO, or from a receiver, partly because in this case the assets were bought at a discount but also because the freehold site had increased in value.

For over twenty years WMAS was involved in up to half a dozen businesses at any time. These were in a variety of trades ranging from engineering, telecommunication and textile manufacture to distribution and retailing. A common feature was that, between the initial purchase and the maturity of the business (marked by a total or partial sale of shares), the value increased by a multiple of the number of years which had elapsed. This happened with both quoted and unquoted companies, in England and in Ireland. In the light of this phenomenon, for which I offer no explanation, the Langdons outcome was not exceptional.

- Grasp a business opportunity but do not overtrade.
- Secure a binding commitment from a new customer before making a significant investment to support the promised business.
- Use experts for specialist engineering or construction work.
- Select new investors who are not impatient or greedy and treat them fairly.
- If you lack resources to carry on your main business and a sideline, discard the sideline.

Chapter 14

MORE EXPANSION AND CASH
BUT LESS SUNNY DELIGHT

The decline in sales of Sunny Delight in the summer of 1999 did not seem to worry the Procter and Gamble team. The launch had attracted wide publicity and it was not surprising that demand was dropping when the process of stock-building in retail outlets had been accomplished. After the initial push, the German managers running the project started looking for ways of reducing costs, and an obvious area was the unnecessary 50-mile shuttle to the store which Langdons was renting from TDG at Willand to supplement its capacity at Walford Cross. To save these wasteful journeys, Michael Donoghue agreed that Langdons would try to provide all the chilled storage space needed for Sunny Delight on one site. There were other amendments to the five-year contract which both sides had agreed, and I had been asked to draft a new agreement incorporating these changes.

Despite having bought from a farmer a three-acre field beside its site at Walford Cross, Langdons had again run out of space on which a warehouse could be built after it had concreted the field for parking and built on the area formerly occupied by the truck stop. There was, however, some land available on the other side of the lane, next to premises occupied by a caravan distributor. The farmer was prepared to sell and it appeared there was a reasonable chance that planning permission would be granted to build warehouses, especially as a proposal had been mooted to relocate the cattle market from the centre of Taunton on other agricultural land nearby.

There were a number of obstacles in the way of developing this property, apart from those routinely raised by the officials working for the local council. A gas main ran below the site and electricity pylons were above it. Because one boundary was adjacent to a motorway, the planners insisted in preliminary discussions that up to two-fifths of the area would have to be devoted to landscaping even though Langdons would have to pay an industrial price for all of it. This stipulation appeared unreasonable because the adjacent land on the other side of a lane, which was already being used for the same purpose, was fully visible to passing motorway traffic. In addition, the undulating levels would have made construction expensive, both of buildings and of parking areas.

One of the conditions of the new Sunny Delight contract was that Langdons would have the new storage facility ready by 1 June 1999. Given the planning delays faced by any industrialist seeking to create wealth and employment through the construction of new buildings (or to despoil the environment, from a different perspective), the time constraint was always going to prove difficult. Having already paid consultants' fees amounting to £18,000 for technical advice, Langdons were about to send the council a cheque for £9,500 when lodging the planning application. On top of that would be an impost levied under Section 106 because the Highway Authority would be sure to demand a contribution towards the cost of yet more improvements to the junction where the cul-de-sac servicing Langdons' site met the main road.

Rob Holder, at that time a non-executive director but still closely watching the cash position, was uneasy about the amount of investment which this further development at Walford Cross would involve. He made enquiries about a 10-acre industrial site near the motorway junction between North Petherton and Bridgwater which had come on the market. A builders' merchant had obtained planning permission to develop the land, but had run into financial difficulties. A developer had bought the property and was now offering it for sale at the same price per acre as the farmer was asking for the agricultural land without planning permission at Walford Cross. Here was somewhere immediately available within a mile of a motorway junction, in the right direction, and located in a district where the council and its officers did not discourage commercial development.

To have any hope of meeting its deadline at Walford Cross, Langdons had to submit its formal planning application to the Taunton Deane Council by 7 September 1998, and hand over the £9,500 fee. As Michael Donoghue was away on a course that day – he was and still is an enthusiastic golfer – I was about to confirm with the architect, Kenneth Steel, that it was all right to sign the cheque and submit the application when he telephoned me at home to say that the planners now wanted an archaeological survey, and were demanding another £12,500 to pay for it. If the archaeologists discovered in the fields a shard of pottery or another significant relic such as a bone, the project would be delayed by at least six months to allow them to dig further. Kenneth already realised that the project was no longer feasible. Even though it might mean splitting its operations, the only way of Langdons honouring the commitment to be operational in a new store within nine months was to look elsewhere.

It was a situation which, in Michael Donoghue's absence, I needed to discuss urgently with Rob Swindells and Paul Rowe. I also needed to leave on Michael's desk the draft of the new contract with Procter and Gamble. When I walked into his office I found Rob Swindells talking to the three senior managers from Hamburg, who had been visiting Gerber in Bridgwater and decided to make an unannounced call on Langdons. I told them that, because of the archaeological survey requirement, it would be impossible to guarantee that a new warehouse would be available at Walford Cross by the following June, but that there was land available in Bridgwater. Their disappointment quickly turned to enthusiasm because, other considerations apart, a store in Bridgwater would save ten miles of shuttle between the factory and Walford Cross, on top of the fifty from there to Willand and back.

I then raised another problem. Within its financial constraints, Langdons could only fund half the cost of buying the land and erecting the building in Bridgwater. They asked us how much we needed. I took a guess and said that, as the total cost would be in the region of £4 million, we would need them to lend us £2 million, which would have to be free of interest and non-repayable until such time as the building might be sold. The accountant among them looked across to his boss, who nodded. That might be possible, we were told, using money already budgeted for the launch but still untouched. From that moment further expansion at Walford Cross was dead, and Langdons became committed to Bridgwater.

Michael Donoghue returned to work the next day to discover that months of negotiation, and a lot of money, to secure the land across the lane had been wasted. He enthusiastically endorsed the decisions Rob Swindells, Paul Rowe and I had taken and turned his attention to buying and developing the new site, which Kenneth Steel's survey revealed to be more than an acre larger than the vendor had thought or charged for and so provided room for a new garage and workshop on site in addition to offices, the warehouse, bunkering, truck wash, and parking.

It was not long before my estimate of the expense of developing the Bridg-water site proved hopelessly optimistic. None of us realised at the time that the nature of the subsoil was such that buildings needed piling because normal foundations would not be sufficient. Constructing the new garage and workshop added another £400,000 to the cost, and the eventual figure amounted to £6.9 million. Having agreed in principle the request for a loan of £2 million, Procter and Gamble suggested without much conviction that £1.5 million might be a figure which was more acceptable to them. Michael Donoghue countered this by saying that, on an investment of more than £6 million, Langdons could not proceed without a subvention of £3 million if it were to stay within the rule that it would not at any time borrow more than the amount of its equity and this was the sum agreed on.

As the loan had been made expressly so that Langdons could build the new facility for the storage and distribution of Sunny Delight, the parties confirmed it would become repayable if Langdons sold the Bridgwater site. The Langdons board and Lloyds Bank looked upon such an interest-free indefinite loan as an injection of capital. The auditors, who were technically correct, insisted that it was a contingent liability which had to be shown as such on the company's balance sheet. The loan remained in place during the five years of the initial Sunny Delight distribution contract. When the parties negotiated a contract to cover the next five years, they agreed that Langdons should return half the money and keep the balance as a payment for services to be rendered and in consideration of amendments to the contract conditions. Thus Langdons

27 *Bridgwater truckwash.*

28 *Bridgwater garage.*

strengthened its balance sheet by £1.5 million, with a corresponding rise in its declared profit, but showed a deterioration in its cash flow of the same amount; and Procter and Gamble in effect recovered £1.5 million of its launch budget.

Thanks to the professionalism of Kenneth Steel and Wilf Dickinson, the Bridgwater complex was ready in May 1999, a few days ahead of the deadline. The official opening was fixed for 12 August when Jorge Montoya, the President of Procter and Gamble Foods, was making a visit, accompanied by his senior managers from Hamburg and Newcastle. Although the relocation had gone smoothly, the sales of Sunny Delight were a long way below the projected figures. After initial favourable press coverage, a number of negative articles began to appear in the national newspapers. In December 1998 a boy's skin had turned orange through drinking too much Sunny Delight, the condition diagnosed as arising from the excessive intake of the beta caratine dye used in the formulation. There followed a succession of articles critical of Sunny Delight, hinting at possibly harmful additives, drawing attention to the supposedly low percentage of fruit juice used in the manufacture, and suggesting that it was not as beneficial to children as might have been thought. Dentists condemned the sugar content, which they said was harmful to the teeth of the young, but without mentioning that other popular fizzy drinks consumed by children were similarly sweetened. It was not exactly knocking copy, but if a competitor had decided to initiate a campaign persistently to damage Sunny Delight over several months it could hardly have done a better job.

When Jorge Montoya and his entourage returned to the board room I asked him how he viewed the adverse publicity that had been appearing in the British press for the past eight months. He turned to his underlings and asked, 'What publicity?' They had not told him about it.

Although a new formulation of the drink reduced the sugar content, Sunny Delight never again achieved the sales experienced immediately after its launch. In 2005 Procter and Gamble sold the business to a private equity firm. Gerber continued to manufacture the product in Bridgwater and Langdons to distribute it, along with other Gerber chilled drinks, but not under a direct contract with the new owner. The 10,000 pallets a week, however, remained a distant memory.

The decline in Sunny Delight sales meant there was space in Bridgwater to relocate the storage, picking and distribution of all Gerber products. For the time being the growing ChillNet operation stayed at Walford Cross, and the vacant space there was rented to a meat processor and to the milk distributor Wiseman Dairies.

When the Bridgwater store had been planned, no provision had been made for offices beyond those needed to manage the store. As the sales of Sunny Delight declined, there was a steady shift in Langdons' activities from Walford Cross to Bridgwater. Operating on a split site separated by five miles is an inconvenient, time-wasting and expensive business involving much cost duplication, but it was not until 2007 that the cam had finally rotated to such an extent that the rump of the Langdons' operation was able to vacate Walford Cross and occupy fine new offices built in Bridgwater. Langdons then sold Walford Cross, generating substantial funds for reinvestment, including the purchase of the depot at Knowsley which had formerly been the headquarters of Tom Granby.

In 2007 Wiseman Dairies, the tenant of most of the Walford Cross store, built its own facility near Langdons in North Petherton and the same year Taunton Market, which might have stayed in Taunton Deane if it had moved to Walford Cross under different circumstances, also joined Langdons and Wiseman near the motorway exit between North Petherton and Bridgwater. When, in September 1998, the Taunton Deane planners learned that Langdons had abandoned its plans to build at Walford Cross, they suggested that the archaeological survey might not be necessary after all. The survey has still not been made and the fields are still agricultural land.

From all of which we may observe the following points:

- Do not be afraid to set what might seem stringent conditions on a contract.
- Do not accept a commitment which may be dependent on the actions of a third party, and especially one needing planning approval.
- Avoid operating from split sites in the same vicinity.
- Tell your superiors bad news as well as good.
- Never forget that managers of private businesses and public servants work under different constraints.

Chapter 15

LANGDONS' TRAFFIC CONTROL AND KEEPING CUSTOMERS HAPPY

The potential damage threatened when the Wiltshire Constabulary raided Langdons on 13 October 1993 will be appreciated by those familiar with the intricacies of traffic control in a complex distribution business. At that time the traffic office recorded its information partly on scraps of paper and other manual forms, without first recording it or backing it up on the IT system. With the loss of the paper records, the business would have come to a standstill and the financial consequences would have been dire.

Apart from the risk that the loss of records involved, the system was flawed in other respects. Pieces of paper get mislaid, especially when there are thousands of them in circulation moving between different offices. Individuals make errors in recording or transcribing information. The system does not automatically draw attention to the fact that something has been overlooked. If it did nothing else which was beneficial, the raid showed Langdons that its IT systems needed urgent upgrading.

At the time of the raid, Langdons' accounting systems were computerised but the firm was using a relatively unsophisticated IT programme to assist its traffic management and was experiencing difficulties in commissioning upgrades on acceptable terms. When the Scottish company Scotfrost joined the ChillNet operation, Langdons became aware of the Mandata IT package and switched to that system. Spencer Dixon and his team in the Langdons' IT department continually adapt and improve the basic system, working with the Mandata staff. This is a topic to which we will return shortly. A decade after the police incursion, the only important pieces of paper remaining in the traffic control system are the PODs – proofs of delivery. Everything else has become controlled by input to the IT systems. If the police had returned in 2007, they would might still have needed many black sacks for the documentation but it would all have been backed up as computer files.

Customer orders reach the traffic office through different routes. The majority arrive by telephone, e-mail or fax. If by telephone, the customer is asked to confirm by one of the other media. Many regular customers are granted limited access to Langdons' IT system and can place their regular orders online. Traffic controllers do not have to discuss prices within the United Kingdom and Ireland because the tariffs are published, indicating the rate for varying quantities of pallets between and within different geographical zones. Where cargo is destined for export to Europe, the traffic controller will obtain a rate from Langdons' German partner, Nagel UK, which is based in Dover. Each established customer has a credit limit and the scrupulous managers in Credit Control keep the traffic offices informed about uncertain credit risks or customers on stop.

Most of the ChillNet chilled produce, having precise sell-by dates, is shipped forward immediately after collection and cross-docking without having to be racked and stored, although some customers, with limited refrigerated storage space of their own, complicate the operation by requesting a delay between collection and delivery. Langdons may, however, store frozen produce for weeks or months, especially in the period leading up to Christmas. The firm issues tariffs of storage rates, although customers specifying a short delay between collection and delivery may not be charged for the storage element even when it involves racking. All costs are calculated by the pallet, even where there may only be individual boxes to be carried, unless special sample rates have been agreed in advance. Each pallet's storage location must be recorded to make sure that the goods on those pallets selected for delivery have the right sell-by credentials and have been kept at the correct temperature.

In the case of the Gerber products, all of which are stored and have to be picked in a separate warehouse, the traffic bookings depend upon the daily demands received direct from Gerber's customers. In this instance the documentation is handled by a dedicated member of the team, Dorothy, or Dot, now Stone and formerly Brown. After being assembled, the Gerber traffic is treated as any other customer delivery and, if less than a full load, consolidated with the ChillNet pallets. As we saw earlier, Dorothy started working for Langdons with Chris Murt in the Avonmouth office, when the business consisted mainly of the onward shipment of frozen lamb and butter from New Zealand. The dockers, operating under the Dock Labour Scheme, were accustomed to unload the cargoes on to the quay and then leave them there until such time as they could transfer them to Langdons' trailers on overtime. The butter was sometimes transported in vehicles which were not temperature-controlled and remained marketable. The lamb was less amenable to such treatment, especially when it had been allowed to defrost in hot weather.

The Irish traffic, shared through Shannon Transport in Limerick and other depots in the Republic, and Sawyers in the North, has also to be handled outside the normal operational structure, mainly because of the sea crossing involved. After his vehicle with its load of meat was stolen from a supermarket in Bridgwater and not seen again, Trevor Searle moved from driving to traffic control and now manages the English element of what has been a fast-growing business, although other pressures on the Limerick team have hitherto prevented the full exploitation of the ChillNet opportunity in the Republic.

As soon as an order is received in the traffic office it is given a job number, which will follow the transaction through to invoicing and payment. This means that the accounting process and information are generated by the operational team and not by accountants at a later stage. There are three different elements to each transaction. The collection leg is handled by one traffic operator, who is responsible for ensuring that the rigid vehicles pick up all the day's orders from within the area covered by the hub. A second traffic operator handles the trunking operation between hubs, ensuring that sufficient vehicles are available every night for what may be a widely varying demand. Another operator is responsible for the outward delivery from the hubs, co-ordinating this operation with the collections being made on their rounds by the same vehicles. When their customer demand is known and the traffic controllers' planning completed, the IT system issues the manifests for the drivers, the trailers or rigids are loaded and the vehicles depart.

Each depot normally has sufficient capacity in its rigid vehicles to handle all its collection and delivery needs. The trunking load is less predictable, with peaks of demand under certain weather conditions or around public holidays. The traffic operator is able to call upon a team of approved sub-contractors, none of whom requires more than 24 hours' notice that he will be needed. Every driver is debriefed by a traffic operator on returning to the depot to check that all PODs have been received and that there have been no rejections or other problems. Relevant information about temperature control throughout the journey, delivery times and so on are automatically recorded for each trip by the IT system.

It is a primary duty of the traffic controller to ensure that no driver exceeds the permitted hours of work without rest periods, and that all journeys are planned accordingly. As we have previously noted, there are occasions, such as motorway blockages, where the driver cannot avoid breaking the law, whether he parks on the hard shoulder or drives on. In those cases the traffic operator checks that the incident has been properly noted in writing on the tachograph – something which will be difficult to do when machine-digital tachographs become standard equipment. The tachographs are passed by the traffic controllers to the company's two dedicated tachograph controllers for further analysis, and then delivered to an independent outside consultant for yet more checking. Any driver who deliberately contravenes the rest period regulations is given a written warning, and if the offence is repeated is dismissed.

As a further safeguard against the temptation to a driver to run a risk over rest periods, all Langdons' drivers, other than the few remaining owner-drivers, are salaried rather than paid hourly. One of the misunderstandings by the Wiltshire police arose because they could not comprehend that a driver taking a rest period a long way from home was still entitled to be paid, and being paid did not *ipso facto* mean that he was not resting. Today a Langdons' driver loses nothing financially by ensuring that he obeys the rules.

If a driver runs out of time and is still away without completing his scheduled work, the traffic operator sends a relief driver by car to take over. Each depot also operates a refrigerated van which is mainly used to make collections or deliveries when, in the warehouse or the traffic office, someone has made a mistake or all the load was not available in time for normal delivery. In allocating tasks to specific vehicles, the operator has to make sure that the one designated is not too large to gain access to the customer's premises. Deliveries within the London conurbation from the Luton depot present especial problems. To handle the difficulty of operating in places such as the mainline railway stations, each vehicle working in the metropolis needs to carry a mate to assist the driver.

The traffic controller must also ensure that the total weight of the tractor, trailer and load is within the permitted limit. In the case of an articulated vehicle with normal loads, this may involve carrying 24 rather than the possible 26 pallets. As trailers may be loaded by warehouse staff employed by another company without the driver having access, or a standing trailer may be picked up later, it is not always possible to ensure that the load is correctly limited on each axle, as required by the regulations. This can lead to unjust punishment. On one occasion, for instance, butter was incorrectly loaded on to a Langdons' trailer by the employees of a dairy in Devon. When the vehicle was checked in Wiltshire, it was found to be correct in total weight but the load wrongly distributed over the axles. As with tachograph errors, the basic principle of *mens rea*, or guilty intent, does not apply to an absolute traffic offence, and although neither the driver nor Langdons could possibly have known or been responsible for the transgression, they were each fined £2,000. The firm and warehouseman who were responsible were not prosecuted.

While many customers are reasonably flexible about collection and delivery times, the RDCs of supermarkets, with their limited loading bays and heavy inward traffic, run what is in effect an appointment system, adding one more complexity to the traffic controller's task. When deliveries are made to the

29 *A manifest.*

RDCs during the day, this gives rise to both an opportunity and a challenge: the opportunity is to double-shift the equipment, trunking by night and then operating by day with a different driver; the challenge is finding a daytime return load after tipping at the RDC. Traffic congestion makes the controller's task yet more complicated when there is a fixed delivery slot, although, as we noted, satellite tracking identifies the constant location of each pallet whether in store or in transit. This enables the traffic controller to advise the RDC of any late arrival and try to obtain a fresh delivery slot.

Anyone seeking to run a business efficiently needs to know the profitability or otherwise of each operation, and of each element within it. Obviously the figures relating to the remaining owner-drivers, paying a commission on their loads but bearing their own tractor cost, have to be separated. Where possible, Langdons also keeps track on the performance of each vehicle, as well as assessing the profitability of each storage operation and of each depot. To do this it has to allocate the transport revenue between collection, trunking and delivery, and this is achieved by arbitrarily dividing the revenue in the ratio of 25 per cent, 25 per cent and 50 per cent. Storage and picking, as with the Gerber product, are charged on an agreed basis. The traffic operator's responsibility only ends when the PODs are passed to Kate Lacey and her administrative department, and the invoices are dispatched.

A good traffic operator has comprehensive geographical knowledge, high IT skills, a formidable memory, commercial acumen and quick intelligence. He, or frequently she, remains calm under pressure and understands the difficulties drivers face. The work is often stressful and never dull. It is, however, an excellent preparation for senior management, as Langdons' experience has shown. At one time or another, all its senior managers on the operational side, apart from Patrick Griffiths and Spencer Dixon, have been traffic operators.

> The Monday after Christmas Day in 1998 was a public holiday on which Michael Donoghue, Rob Swindells, Paul Rowe, Chris Murt, Arran Osman and other managers were not working. Aware that retailers would be replenishing their stocks after the holiday trade and living nearby, I walked up to Walford Cross to see how the depleted team was getting on. Between 11 that morning and 4 p.m. when I left they had selected or cross-docked 1,381 pallets and dispatched 116 vehicles, without a single error. With staff like that, who needs managers?

- Publish your rate schedules and stick to them.
- Select and use reliable sub-contractors.
- Ensure that drivers can achieve their task within the permitted hours.
- Monitor individual profit centres down to each store and vehicle.
- Debrief every driver after every shift.
- Work for a spell as a traffic operator if you want to become a senior manager.

Chapter 16
LANGDONS' ACCOUNTS AND BUDGETS

Figures are the language of business. The one hard fact they tell us is how much cash we have or how much we owe. Businesses do not necessarily fail because they are not profitable. They fail when they run out of money. Accounts may record accurately what has happened, but that is their least important function. They may also relate what is happening currently, which is important. Their essential value, however, if we use them correctly, is to advise or warn us of what is likely to happen in the future.

David Every-Clayton, the person responsible for producing the accounts in Langdons, is not a 'bean-counter' but a monitor, ensuring that any abnormality in the planned operating performance of any part of the business is immediately noted and investigated. David is a pragmatist, someone whose glass is usually half empty, and reluctant to accept any specious explanation about a figure which he did not expect. The 43 pages of accounts which his department generates each month and passes, with appropriate comments, to each senior manager, probe every aspect of the business. Nobody studies these accounts with greater skill and advantage than Michael Donoghue himself. Although Michael may gain gratification, or otherwise, from the reported profit, the schedule to which he also pays close attention is the one which shows the company's actual and projected cash position. As we have noted before, in the realm of business, cash is king.

Budgeting has to be the precursor to the preparation of accounts for any period, the foundation on which the structure is built and the standard against which performance is monitored. In a sense, therefore, the accounting calendar does not start with David Every-Clayton's input, or even that of Simon Holder, whose duties involve being the part-time Financial Director. Nothing would be more perilous than allowing accountants to prepare a budget on spread-sheets based on broad percentage assumptions and letting the computer convert them into projections. That practice saves a lot of time, thought, and contention – you watch the machine-generated figures dance across the screen and print them out. You want more profit? Easy. Raise the gross margin by 1 per cent. Regrettably the future is never so simple and the elements which make up a business do not wax and wane, increase and decrease, in even patterns or at the same rate.

Long before the financial year begins, every senior manager in Langdons works with the Managing Director on preparing the draft budget to be put before the board for the following year. Because those responsible for the performance of each profit centre help to prepare the budget, they also remain responsible for delivering the result. In budget preparation (and the absence of crystal balls), thought and experience are the essential ingredients. There are customers who may be won or lost, competitors who threaten parts of the operation or leave a gap in the market, company facilities which are inadequate or under-utilised, people who are retiring or to be recruited, costs which are impossible to predict, vehicle repairs, hire-purchase payments, capital investments, insurance premiums – the list seems endless, and each item has to be individually considered, argued over and agreed before the budget process is completed and the accountants' work of converting the implications into figures can begin. Then, when the cash flow is unsatisfactory or the profit too low, the process has to be refined until every bit of the jigsaw falls into place and the puzzle is completed.

In any business, nothing happens until you sell something, whether goods or services. The first input to the budget therefore comes from the commercial team, especially Rob Swindells and Rupert Ryall in Bridgwater, and Chris Davies in Liverpool. Which customer accounts are under threat? (The salesmen will suggest that they all are, because their task is less daunting when prices are kept low, and they want to scotch any suggestion of putting them up.) Having made their ritual warning about the hard times ahead, they will give a realistic assessment of threats and opportunities, and the resources they will need to counter or take advantage of them. Knowing that, in the Department of Transport's 2007 evaluation of loading factors among national hauliers, Langdons was rated the most efficient operator in the country, they remain confident that it is virtually impossible for a competitor to undercut the company's rates and provide a similar service. Then, having exhausted the topic of transport threats and opportunities, they give their view on storage capacity, where it is needed and how divided between sub-zero and chilled, and on what new customers must be found so that the warehouses are fully used.

Armed with this sales forecast, Arran Osman's emphasis shifts to equipment. Spencer Dixon needs comprehensive IT facilities if the depots are to generate and use information to the best advantage. IT equipment and software are expensive and both need constant upgrading. As the number of depots increases along with the volume of trade, Spencer may not need more staff but he needs more terminals, which means more licence fees. Next come Graham Millard, Trevor Horton and the transport experts. How many vehicles will be needed to meet the projected turnover? Where will they be based? Which trailers have become too costly to maintain and should be traded on? Which prime movers are coming up for replacement? Where transport equipment is concerned, the depreciation will probably go a long way towards offsetting the capital costs but the figures still have to be calculated. (We will be looking in more detail at how Spencer Dixon and Graham Millard organise their departments in due course.)

More weighty issues may arise, such as the acquisition of a new depot: where it should be located and whether to rent or buy, and if bought, whether to build or to adapt an existing structure. The strategic location of depots can only be decided after detailed analysis of traffic patterns and projected customer needs. As the business grows, it becomes more economical for each hub to serve a smaller area because its rigids have more work to get through on their daily drop and collection routine. Opening a new depot involves an operating loss of at least £150,000 before it breaks even, without taking into account the capital investment which even leased premises usually require. This is something on which the board must make the final decision because, as the company places no value on intangible assets such as goodwill and writes off improvements quickly, the start-up costs will impair current profit as well as impacting the cash flow.

The budget team then moves on to people. As we have already noted, costs walk on two feet, but without bipeds there is no business. What will be the annual wage increase and for how many staff? There are bound to be shortages of drivers from time to time. How much do we budget for agency drivers, and how much for sub-contractors? How much will we need to spend on training? What will it cost to replace a key member of the team who is coming up to retirement or wants to start working part-time?

When the trading assumptions have been made, David Every-Clayton can calculate the cash effect. If debtors have been paying at an average of 56 days, say, he can forecast how much more cash the increased turnover will absorb. With bad debts running at around £100,000 a year, a reserve for them of £10,000 a month should suffice. If capital investment cannot be met from disposals, depreciation and profit, the board will have to decide whether or not to spend the money, and then how to finance it, because working capital must never be touched for capital projects. At that stage, Michael Donoghue, Simon Holder, Arran Osman and Pat Griffiths will sit down with David Gale of Lloyds Bank, or someone in his place, and discuss the financial consequences of what is being proposed. With two decades of uncannily accurate budgeting behind them, the management team and the banker know that any error is likely to be on the conservative side. When selecting the provider of hire-purchase on vehicles the company goes to the lowest bidder, but for capital projects stays with its trusty bank.

After Langdons became, as we will see shortly, a subsidiary of the Nagel Group, whose headquarters are based in Germany, the final act in the budgeting process is for the directors to present the end product to the Nagel Group in Versmold. As any key issue such as buying a new depot will have been discussed previously, the budget presentation is normally a formality, and after watching its English subsidiary for three years or more the Nagel Group has learnt that it is as meticulous in its budget preparation as it is in its financial reports.

Following the cerebral exercise of budgeting, the preparation of monthly accounts may seem tame, and it is here that the computers prove their worth. The accounts show the actual result alongside the budgetary assumptions, and also provide comparatives for the previous year. The costs are also expressed in percentage terms so that variances can be quickly spotted. As you may have already gathered, each item of expense is available, down to tyre usage on individual prime movers and repairs to each trailer. With only two remaining owner-drivers, their accounts are no longer the concern and cash drain of the early years, but that does not obviate the need for the minute examination of fuel consumption and repair costs for every vehicle in the fleet. Whatever David Every-Clayton fails to spot, which is very little, Michael Donoghue, Simon Holder, Pat Griffiths or Arran Osman will pick up. And if they all missed it, the Nagel Group, which uses the SAP IT system for its financial control, would detect it. In Langdons things cannot go wrong for much longer than a month before they are noticed and action is taken to recover the situation.

There are, I am sure, lengthy and learned academic tomes describing the process of spotting discrepancies between forecast and performance in accounts, or management by exception. The wisdom of setting targets and assessing probabilities, and then examining regularly anything which moves out of phase, is such obvious common sense and good commercial practice that we need not dilate upon it further. The accounts should not contain any information which is not necessary for the management and control of the business nor should any figures be circulated to managers which are not comprehensible to all those who have to use them. (Deferred tax may be the exception to this rule as the calculation is probably incomprehensible to everyone but trained accountants and the auditors. As the Revenue changes the rules every now and then, and deferred tax is not a cash item, we can make that one exception.)

Taxation is a massive burden on all industry but especially on a British transport company which does not have the advantage its Irish and continental competitors enjoy of filling their tanks abroad before travelling the highways of the United Kingdom. Perhaps a third of Langdons' expenditure is on fuel, with diesel more expensive than anywhere else in the developed world because around 80 per cent of the cost is tax. That means that on a turnover of £1 million a month around £250,000 is paid in duty on fuel alone. Large Goods Vehicle (LGV) road licences vary from £700 to £1,200 a year. Every item of equipment bought for the business is subject to Value Added Tax, involving a massive quarterly payment of the net sum due to the Revenue. Wages are subject to Income Tax up to 51 per cent, some of which is called, or disguised as, National Health Insurance. Insurance premiums are taxed. And so it goes. Apart from baby clothes, books and food, in the United Kingdom, if you are not a professional politician, everything is taxed.

As we noted earlier, a company can legitimately do certain things to minimise tax by taking advantage of concessions such as investment allowances, but not much. All the taxes, apart from Corporation Tax, have to be passed on to customers by incorporating them in the pricing structure, and so eventually, with Langdons, to the general public in the cost of food. The budgeting process is not complete until the tax burden has been calculated and included in the projected cash flow.

With wide fluctuations in the cost of fuel, it is imperative that any time-lag in recovering or allowing their effect on tariffs should be minimised. Langdons buys fuel at spot prices on a daily basis and varies the fuel surcharge on prices every fortnight. As the company has its own bunkering facilities at its depots, the two–week cycle eliminates an element of risk and is fair on the customers. It also means that, even if the budgetary estimates of diesel prices are wrong, the credit and debit items on the profit and loss account remain at the same ratio.

From the first day of the MBO in 1986 Langdons moved into profit and managed its cash within agreed limits. That was possible because Rob Holder and Paul Rowe set the tone, David Every-Clayton and his team understand the business, and his fellow managers understand the relevance of the figures David produces. From all this we can learn the following lessons:

- Involve those responsible for profit centres in the budgeting process.
- Beware of relying on spread-sheets when you prepare budgets.
- Publish monthly accounts in a form which makes it easy to detect anomalies.
- Do not circulate management accounts in a way or with information which some of the managers may not understand.
- Do not use working capital or overdraft facilities for long-term investment.
- Explain your budgetary plans to your banker and listen to his advice.
- Give credit to your accountancy staff for their contribution to the success of the business.

Chapter 17

LOOKING AFTER PEOPLE

It seems almost a formality in any Chairman's Statement to include a paragraph towards the end thanking the employees for their contribution to the success or otherwise of the business. As we have already observed, without people there is no business and all employees are important because otherwise they shouldn't be on the payroll. Clearly, to secure the right staff and recognise levels of responsibility, competence and application, there have to be different levels of pay, but in Langdons that does not mean that the interests or welfare of any one employee are less important than of another. Possibly because all the senior managers in Langdons were once employed in less responsible jobs within the industry, they appreciate that everyone in the company matters and the corollary, that everyone should make a contribution according to his or her best ability. 'Sickies' and 'duvet days' are discouraged, not least because of the unfair load they place on others.

Immediately after the MBO Langdons had in effect only two sites, at Walford Cross and Arnos Castle, and about 150 employees. At Walford Cross Michael Donoghue always left his door open unless he had a visitor from outside the company, and even then I have seen him break off his discussion to talk to a driver who dropped by for a few words. If he wasn't at his desk, you would be sure to find him in the traffic office, the workshops, the warehouse, or somewhere on the site. The same was true of Rob Swindells at Arnos Castle, while Paul Rowe was equally accessible to everyone. There came a time, however, when the number of employees reached more than 650, many of them located in distant depots, and geography as well as size ruled out such informal personal contacts on a daily basis. It then became important that the relationship between managers and those responsible for personnel issues retained the same respect for the individual as had been a characteristic of Langdons when it was a smaller firm.

Sheila Burnett, aided by Jackie Hampton and others, is the Personnel Manager and is based in Bridgwater. Sheila was originally the secretary to Philip Langdon and then to Michael Donoghue, and it was she who had the unenviable task of typing Philip's letters to TKM complaining about her new boss. Sheila was always much more than just a secretary or personal assistant, although her official appointment as Personnel Manager, recognising a role she had gradually assumed, did not happen until January 1999. By that time, with the advent of personal computers, very few managers in the private sector were not typing their own letters and e-mails, relying heavily at first on two fingers and the spell-check.

Sheila's job does not cover recruitment, which is handled by the manager of the function involved. She issues employment contracts, runs the wages department and ensures that disciplinary procedures are correctly followed. She is also responsible for ensuring that the company complies with all the complex rules relating to discrimination in recruitment. In the private sector, where a single employee may perform a unique function in the business and the service to customers must be maintained at all times, engaging and keeping the right staff is a matter of great importance. It is inevitable that some applicants might be tempted to try to abuse the system by being more concerned with employee's rights than duties. Failing to check such behaviour is both wasteful and unfair on other members of the team. Evidence of Langdons' policy of avoiding discrimination is shown by the fact that it employs many women in senior management positions.

The problem of alleged discrimination may be indicated by what happened when the firm took over the Dover depot from Nagel UK. To improve the efficiency of the operation, it was necessary, among other things, to introduce better use of staff. In one department, five people, three of them women, were doing the work of two if properly organised. All five were asked to apply for the new jobs, to which two of the women were appointed, with the others, including the two men, being made redundant. One of these was a single mother who claimed sexual discrimination on the grounds, we may suppose, that the new conditions would not be convenient for looking after her child or children, and made it unreasonable for her to apply for the new job. It is difficult to conceive that there could have been discrimination on sexual grounds when both posts had gone to women but I am sure it was possible to find a lawyer who took a different view.

Repeated minor tachograph errors lead to a disciplinary hearing and, if they persist, to verbal and written warnings. If the driver is still unable to comply with the rules, he loses his job. Tampering illegally with a tachograph is so serious that the driver has to go immediately. Any offence involving theft or dishonesty also involves instant dismissal, as does assault on another employee. It is part of Sheila's job to see that every disciplinary incident, including an interview between the traffic manager and a driver over a tachograph query, is properly recorded. To ensure that employee rights are fully protected, Sheila may sometimes review the circumstances with Simon Holder, who is experienced in employment law, or with Pat Griffiths, and her department has an open line to a solicitor who specialises in this.

Half of Langdons' employees are Large Goods Vehicle (LGV) drivers, who have to pass a stringent examination and undergo regular medical check-ups as a condition of holding an LGV licence. In addition, the company provides instruction at every depot for all drivers joining the firm. All fork-lift truck drivers have to attend a course and pass an external examination before obtaining their licence. Middle managers attend training courses run by local technical colleges. With a broad – some would say excessively broad – variety of degree courses available, and so many employment opportunities for graduates in an industry without which society as we know it would collapse within days, it may seem remarkable that so few universities offer a specific degree in transport and distribution, even if they chose to name it Logistic Studies. Such a curriculum would include, among other things, geography, mechanical engineering, traffic law, IT and computer science, and personnel management, nor would there be any shortage of openings for on-the-job training for those doing sandwich courses.

Langdons has not hitherto suffered managerially from the paucity of specialist graduates and none of those whose names have featured in this account attended a university. With more people now entering tertiary education, however, it may be less feasible in future years to find young intelligent non-graduates to become the managers of the future.

We have already noted that Glan Robottom chose to continue working after the normal retirement age, as did Dot Stone. Some drivers also keep up their LGV licences when they retire, and make themselves available for casual work. Conversely, those who wish to do so may have the option to reduce their working hours or days before full retirement, which Michael Donoghue, Paul Rowe and Rob Swindells have elected to do as the next generation of senior managers takes over.

Sheila Burnett and her team liaise closely with Ken Bilsborough and his staff, who are responsible for the health and safety of employees who work in an environment fraught with risk of accident or injury. I deliberately did not write 'Health and Safety', because that term has unfortunate connotations, acquired not because of the implicit good sense of the regulations but through the lack of common sense among some of the officials appointed to enforce them.

Ken has the right accreditation for his job in a company like Langdons. After an engineering apprenticeship, he worked in manufacturing before taking a job with a local authority on health and safety. His overriding concern is to prevent accidents. Apart from seeking to ensure that employees use safe working practices, he also conducts training courses. When an industrial rather than a road accident occurs, often caused by lifting, it is part of Ken's remit to protect the interests of both the employee and the company. As people who suffer injury at work have three years in which to decide whether or not to make a claim, during which time public-spirited lawyers will be pleading to become involved in litigation on their behalf without charging a fee, the keeping of accurate records is of the utmost importance.

Health and Safety has acquired its dire reputation with many employers because the Common Law misdemeanours of barratry, maintenance and champerty are no longer enforced. A barrator, or in effect a trouble-maker, is someone who repeatedly instigates legal actions without good cause. Maintenance is the offence of becoming involved in someone else's legal action by funding or supporting it without due cause. Champerty is an extension of Maintenance, the offence being committed when the interfering party has a financial interest in the outcome of the case. The lapse of these safeguards against vexatious or coercive litigation would be less damaging if courts applied the principle that costs go with the cause, but that rarely happens, especially in hearings by industrial tribunals. If losing litigants, their trades union or their lawyers had to pay the defendant's costs, there would have been far fewer than the 132,577 cases heard by the tribunals in 2006/7, and some of the 88 per cent of claimants who failed, or their sponsors, might have paused before going before a tribunal. On the other hand, employees rightly have access to justice against a wealthier defendant.

Because companies know that tribunal hearings will be costly and wasteful of management time, the tendency is to pay the complainant to go away, even if the case has little merit. The Advice and Conciliation Service does its best to winnow out claims which should never be brought but some lawyers are not so scrupulous in their advice to clients. There is also a risk that, despite its best endeavours, an accident or even the supposed threat of an accident may involve the company in a criminal prosecution. The following examples illustrate the legislative environment in which business has to be conducted:

30   *Ken Bilsborough.*

A female employee complained that the chair she was using caused her backache. Langdons took advice from orthopaedic health and safety experts and supplied the chair they recommended. That, too, gave her backache and so she brought her own chair to work. If she had been told to find another job which did not involve sitting all day, she would have had a claim for constructive or wrongful dismissal, and so the company was unable to suggest that as a possible remedy for her medical condition. When she left the firm, Langdons received a claim from her lawyer for a sum approaching £250,000 on the grounds that it was the company's fault that she would never be able to work again. It transpired that the claimant's medical condition preceded her joining Langdons.

When the Varma paper trade was running down, two store men at Arnos Castle lost their regular Saturday morning overtime. They thereupon decided it was too dangerous to unload reels of paper from containers because the load might have shifted. After six weeks' deliberation, an official from the Health and Safety Executive came up with a solution. The containers should be packed in a way which involved their being kept level in transit. As they came from Finland by sea, a copy of his recommendation should have gone to Neptune.

In 2000 Taunton Deane Council Health and Safety officers demanded the delineation by painting of pedestrian paths in the lorry park at Walford Cross. Access to the lorry park was guarded from the public and unauthorised entry prevented by a barrier manned at all times by a security guard. Langdons responded by asking the officials which of their own vehicle parks they should inspect so that they might follow best practice. None of the council parks, to which the public had free access at all times, had marked pedestrian lanes even though some were used by lorries, private cars, parents with pushchairs, toddlers, skateboarders and the like. Langdons were still obliged to spend hundreds of pounds on unnecessary road paint for unused walkways.

On another routine visit the inspectors from Taunton Deane, unhappy perhaps over the pedestrian lane exchange, noted in the warehouse some pallets from abroad which were damaged and of inferior quality. Langdons' fork lift drivers had instructions not to place sub-standard pallets on racks and to withdraw them from use. A subsequent inspection by inspectors on 5 July 2001 revealed a pallet on a rack with a broken rail. The pallet was designed to hold 2 tonnes but was at the time carrying less than 200 kilos. After various changes of indictment, on 3 October 2002 Taunton Deane Council took Langdons to court for failing to ensure the health and safety at work of employees on the spurious ground that the pallet was dangerous. Michael Donoghue said in evidence that, in 22 years of operations using pallets, the firm had not had a single accident. It safely handled thousands of pallets a day although it did not, as suggested by the inspectors, keep a written record every time a faulty pallet was removed from service. All this was in vain, and for one slightly defective pallet rail, which was not unsafe, the firm was fined £2,000 with prosecution costs of £2,049.

> In the early days of ChillNet, Michael Donoghue as Managing Director and I as Chairman took two bottles of champagne to celebrate with the team at Walford Cross their achieving a certain landmark – perhaps 1,000 pallets in a week or some similar significant figure. Michael opened the first bottle and the cork hit the roof. I pointed the second bottle at the staff and asked, 'Who was it who called the Chairman a boring old fart?' Rupert Ryall replied, 'You've only got one bottle.'

Personnel management, employee health and safety, and compliance with regulations require constant and close attention. The following are things to bear in mind:

- Keep meticulous records of anything to do with personnel matters.
- Provide or ensure adequate training facilities for all employees.
- Do not upset unnecessarily inspecting officials however unreasonable or officious they may be.
- Beware of employing serial discrimination or health claimants.
- Never overlook anyone who performs well in a junior function.
- Avoid industrial tribunals and litigation if at all possible.
- Remember that any employee who is not important should not be on the payroll.

Chapter 18

CHOOSING AND LOOKING AFTER EQUIPMENT

It is a truism that a transport company can only operate efficiently if its employees are provided with tools which enable them to perform their duties in a safe and cost-effective way. That means that, in the case of Langdons, the vehicles the drivers use must be reliable and economical, the pallet racking and fork-lift trucks in the cold stores adequate to allow the store men to handle the exacting demands of the ChillNet operation, and the IT systems simple to operate and capable of providing accurate information with minimal input. The choice of vehicles is part of Graham Millard's responsibility, Chris Murt looks after the warehouses, and Spencer Dixon advises on all IT matters. As having the right equipment is so essential to the company's success, it is worth noting how they reach their decisions.

Graham Millard, you may recall, joined Langdons as Fleet Engineer in November 1999 when Barrie Hargreaves retired. He had learned his trade as a vehicle mechanic and had risen to become engineering manager of a large fleet. The Bridgwater depot houses Langdons' own workshop operations and the refrigeration company Marshall Thermo King maintains a repair and inspection facility there with two of its own employees. The tyre factor ATS also keeps an employee permanently on the site. Although there is a national shortage of skilled vehicle and diesel fitters, Trevor Horton, who is in charge of the garage, has little difficulty in attracting and keeping good mechanics. There are four clerical staff, including David Strathdee and Paul Whitehead. Their tasks include monitoring the fuel consumption, tyre wear and incidence of repairs for each vehicle, using a Tranman IT package, which is not linked to Spencer Dixon's Mandata. Paul also orders spare parts and maintains the stores. To make sure he is aware of any unusual or exceptional costs, Graham sees and approves every invoice himself before passing it for payment.

David Strathdee is also responsible for ensuring that every prime mover and trailer is returned to Bridgwater when it is due to undergo its periodic Ministry of Transport test at the Vehicle Testing Station in Taunton. Bringing the equipment back to Bridgwater enables Trevor Horton and his team to inspect everything that has been repaired or is being maintained by third parties at other depots, and so to assess the performance of the garage which has been chosen to do the work.

31 *Graham Millard.*

Graham Millard handles the daily ordering of diesel fuel and makes the recommendations for the choice of new prime movers and trailers, including the preparation of detailed specifications. Every day he receives information about fuel levels in each depot, and ten or more quotations from suppliers. While he is happy to try out motive equipment from a reputable supplier on a trial basis, until something better emerges he divides his purchases of prime movers between three manufacturers, Renault, DAF and Scania. Langdons no longer transfers the refrigerated body from an old rigid chassis to the new one when the prime mover element needs replacing, but it still uses its long-term supplier Gray and Adams for all its trailers as well as the rigid bodies. Many tractors are bought from the manufacturer with a guaranteed price on buy-back in three years' time. This does more than remove any risk of loss on resale: it means that for all or much of their lives, the tractors are under warranty from the manufacturer. Where the tractor has done mostly single-shift work, Langdons may keep it up to five years, as it does with most rigids.

Graham is acutely aware of the need to reduce vehicle emissions as far as possible, on environmental grounds, apart from the vehicle tax incentives which are available. Two systems of reducing emissions are currently available, Exhaust Gas Recycling (EGR), which is self-explanatory, and Selective Catalytic

32 *Loading bays at Bridgwater.*

Reduction (SCR), under which additives are fed into the exhaust system to reduce the emissions. Langdons currently uses SCR rather than EGR. The adoption of either system reduces the annual licence fee for each 44-tonne artic by £500. With increased public awareness of the effect of emissions on the climate, and the involvement of the European Community, the industry faces more stringent regulation from Brussels, which may well have the effect of driving old or badly maintained vehicles off the road. Reducing the total number of miles travelled is also relevant, which is why maintaining a high vehicle loading factor is not just good commercial practice.

Langdons' vehicles mainly carry food and drink. The simple, pure, blue and white livery, with its striking letters and ChillNet roundel, is the advertisement millions of motorists have the chance of seeing on the roads every day. If the equipment is clean, that is a good advertisement; if dirty, not so good. That is why it is imperative to keep the truck wash in Bridgwater and other cleaning facilities elsewhere in good working order. If the vehicles on the road are not in their usual pristine condition, you can guess that Trevor Horton is having trouble with his truckwash again.

The garage staff do not maintain the fork-lift trucks. Chris Murt, who is in charge of the storage operations, makes recommendations to Arran Osman about what equipment is needed, and then negotiates a purchase from one of three suppliers, Linde, Atlet and Jungheinrich, entering into a contract for the manufacturer to undertake maintenance and repair. Langdons keeps the trucks for five years and then trades them in with the supplier. By buying the trucks rather than leasing them, the company avoids being left with redundant equipment should the pattern of demand change. Chris also manages the purchase and lay-out of the pallet racking in the stores. It is part of his responsibility to inspect regularly the condition of racking and the pallets in the stores in each depot and to ensure that all store men and fork-lift drivers detect and report any damage. If a pallet is defective in any respect, pending disposal it must not be placed on a rack but left on the ground.

When Spencer Dixon joined Langdons as IT Manager in 1997, his predecessor, Roger Donoghue, had already introduced an IT system called Roadrunner which was being used by Langdons for handling transport operations where loads were carried between two fixed points, rather than shared-user work such as ChillNet. Spencer's first priority was to create a database for the ChillNet service which printed labels for individual pallets; these were being written by hand, a time-consuming and error-prone procedure. Following on from the pallet printing, Spencer developed what became known as the ChillNet Database. This produced notes of goods received and vehicle manifests, in addition to providing movement information which was helpful to traffic controllers.

With the rapid growth of ChillNet, and the participation of partners such as Tom Granby, it became increasingly inefficient to run Roadrunner and the ChillNet Database in parallel. It was also a nightmare for people like Kate Lacey who were faced with re-keying the ChillNet data into the Roadrunner database and then manually pricing all the ChillNet work, using in those days a complex schedule based on mileage from the collecting depot. The procedure relied on the transfer of information on paper, which is often mislaid or incorrectly prepared. With an imperfect IT system, traffic controllers had often been unable to calculate the price for a job, which put even more work on to the administrative staff. Customers who were overcharged demanded credits, others were undercharged or not charged at all, and there were constant financial queries between Langdons and the other companies participating in ChillNet which Paul Rowe had to spend a great deal of effort resolving.

By the summer of 1999 Rob Swindells had become exasperated by the time he and Rupert Ryall were spending placating ChillNet customers, and the damage the inefficient administration was doing to the business. The administrative staff were equally frustrated at constantly having to sort out the mistakes which were inevitable given the inadequacies of the IT systems. To resolve the problem, Michael Donoghue asked Spencer Dixon and Patrick Griffiths to think the unthinkable and come up with a radical solution. Spencer and Patrick started by producing a draft flow-chart for all the processes involved in a ChillNet transaction, from order receipt, through keying in, planning, vehicle manifest, pallet labelling, POD control, pricing and invoicing, to payment by the customer. As they consulted with those involved, it became apparent that additional information was needed, such as the vehicle used, the transport partner involved, and so on. The final and agreed draft flow-chart, numbered 53, was produced in October 1999. It was then time to locate or produce an IT system which met all the demands for the generation of data indicated on the flow-chart.

In their search for a solution, Spencer and Patrick first went to Knowsley to see how Tom Granby managed their equally complex problems, and discovered that they were little better placed than Langdons. Discussions about upgrading Roadrunner were disappointing, because the software available did not provide the solutions which they were seeking. Then Chris Murt suggested that the two should take a look at the Mandata system being used by Scotfrost. When they examined Mandata's Manpack 2, it appeared to offer much of what they wanted, although with certain limitations. Fortunately the Mandata engineers were working in Newcastle on a new edition, Manpack 3, a programme with a Windows format and a powerful SQL database behind it. Although Mandata 3 was not yet in service, it promised to provide everything Spencer and Patrick were looking for, combining the functions which were being performed unsatisfactorily by Roadrunner and the ChillNet Database. Just as Spencer and Patrick were delighted to have discovered Mandata, Mandata were equally glad to have a potential customer like Langdons, with two talented and enthusiastic IT engineers to help them develop their system. It was to be a great partnership.

The first person in the first haulier to use the Manpack 3 software in a live operation was Arran Osman when, on Thursday 11 January 2001, he entered into the system for a ChillNet customer the carriage of a pallet from Avonmouth to Romsey. During the first few days of operation, the traffic controllers complained about having to key in jobs they had already planned on paper. By the end of the following week, however, the paper had disappeared and the staff had learned how convenient it was to plan their schedules as they keyed in the jobs. They were also finishing work and getting home earlier. Although bits of software constantly had to be rewritten, the changeover was free of problems. It was done on time and on budget, for which Spencer, Patrick, their team and the Mandata staff deserve great credit.

There are, as you would expect, constant improvements to Langdons' IT systems. POD scanning has now been linked with the transport software, reducing the clerical chore of visually checking each of the differently sized pieces of paper, with their non-standard formats, and easing verification. Approved customers can enter orders directly on to the Langdons' website, track their consignments and view PODs and invoices. The keying in of an order generates a bar code which identifies all the documentation for that particular order through to final payment. Spencer notes that, having devised a foolproof paperless system, his users now like to see printed reports, and remarks ruefully, 'The Holy Grail of the paperless office has had the opposite effect!' He is also aware of the danger of producing too much information. That does not, however, prevent him seeking further applications for the IT system which he and Mandata have produced together.

Future developments may include giving customers the facility to locate individual pallets and check temperatures in real time. Visual job mapping would allow a traffic controller to see the incidence of collections and deliveries in any area. Booking precise slots for collection and delivery could be automated, based on the location and estimated time of arrival of the vehicle. The system could also provide better historical information on issues such as drivers' hours, fuel drawings and mileages. Like Graham Millard, Spencer is conscious of the need for improved control of exhaust emissions, and the IT aspect of that issue will need to be addressed when, as seems likely, the actual exhaust emissions of individual vehicles have to be recorded.

Meanwhile, Graham Millard has to keep the fleet operational, Chris Murt ensure that the stores run smoothly, and Spencer Dixon provide a flawless IT system, which leads us to certain conclusions:

- Do not delegate key responsibilities such as fuel purchases.
- Limit the types of equipment bought to avoid excessive spares holdings.
- Do not let the person delegated with the responsibility for purchasing approve invoices for payment.
- Periodically check maintenance carried out by third parties.
- Stay with and work with a reliable supplier.
- Have relevant statistics available, and study them.
- Recognise the importance of IT in your business.
- Regularly make a formal inspection of pallet racking.

Chapter 19

MARKETING AND MANAGEMENT

Rob Swindells, Rupert Ryall and Chris Davies are primarily concerned with introducing new users of ChillNet and making sure that existing customers have reason to be satisfied with the services which Langdons and the other participants provide. The days of cold calling on prospective users of the service are distant memories. The most effective salesmen of ChillNet are the firms already using it, who recommend it to others. The 12 hubs in the United Kingdom and Ireland, and the relationship with the Nagel Group in continental Europe, mean that ChillNet routinely predicts delivery times, offers fixed prices and provides a geographical coverage which no competitor can match. Ten years earlier, things were very different.

We first met Michael Redmond, who was managing Tom Granby, when his company was the tenant of the late, unlamented, temperature-controlled store at Arnos Castle. Tom Granby's headquarters were at Knowsley, near Liverpool, and the company was under contract to make daily deliveries of food and drink throughout the United Kingdom, including provisioning all railway catering services. To achieve this, in addition to the facilities in Knowsley and Bristol, Tom Granby rented space in a depot at Luton from TDG and used Scotfrost, based near Glasgow, for its deliveries into Scotland. We have seen how Langdons took over the work in the South West, when Tom Granby gave up the TDG warehouse in Avonmouth which it had rented after leaving Arnos Castle. Langdons had also taken over the trunking between Tom Granby's hubs other than Knowsley and Luton, so that Tom Granby's fleet consisted mainly of rigid vehicles.

After giving up its articulated vehicles and its depot at Avonmouth, Tom Granby had neither the scale nor the resources to operate its vehicle fleet efficiently. It was also hampered by having to rely on expensive and inflexible contract hire rather than buying the rigids outright. The deal agreed in 1999 whereby Langdons took over all the transport side of Tom Granby, including its rigids and their drivers, proved an unsatisfactory compromise. There had always been issues regarding who was liable for claims when a customer's consignment had been handled by more than one ChillNet member. That allocation of responsibility for damage or error became even more complex and contentious when the two Tom Granby hubs, Knowsley and Luton, were operating the warehouses but no longer using their own transport.

In 2002 Michael Redmond sold Tom Granby to its major customer, the Danish Bacon Company (DBC). The new owners had more pressing interests than developing their participation in ChillNet and agreed that it would be better if Langdons took over all the ChillNet operation, including the hubs in Knowsley and Luton and the invoicing of customers. The wheel came full circle in 2008 when Langdons bought the Knowsley site from DBC.

To provide better cover for the East Midlands, Langdons had set up a depot in a TDG site at Peterborough in 2000. After it had opened the Redditch depot in 2004, most of the southern half and the north-west of England were covered by its own hubs. Scotfrost was still handling Scotland, albeit under two or three changes of ownership and now trading as DHL/Exel. Ireland and the north-east of England were being covered by other members of the consortium based in Limerick, Roscommon, Moy in County Armagh and Wallsend in Northumberland.

One of the Irish partners, Shannon Transport, or STL Logistics as it prefers to be called, started trading in 1972 in the city of Limerick. Two years later it moved its operations to a 14-acre site outside the city on the Tipperary Road. In addition to its modern facilities and headquarters at Annacotty Business Park near Limerick, the company now operates depots in Dublin, Roscommon and Carrigfergus. Under the leadership of its Managing Director, Michael O'Riordan, the son of one of the founders, STL has won many leading British, American and Irish customers for storage and delivery of ambient, chilled and frozen goods. Shannon Transport became a member of ChillNet in 1990 and, although the ChillNet service in Ireland is not yet fully developed, Michael and his co-director Denis Hocter appreciate the potential for giving the many small food producers in the Republic the sales options that ChillNet provides for their counterparts in England, Scotland and Wales. It frees them from dependence on a wholesaler or a co-operative to reach the wider market.

The ChillNet partner in Northern Ireland is another family firm, Sawyers Transport. Derek Sawyer started the business in 1970 and bought his first refrigerated trailer in 1982. Sawyers operates its temperature-controlled warehouse at Moy and now has 80 twin evaporator trailers (which allow the load to be split between chilled and sub-zero) as well as 20 rigids. Like STL, Sawyers sees the potential ChillNet provides for a growing volume of traffic in dairy, meat and other produce between the Province and the rest of the United Kingdom.

The associate who has handled the North East since 2001 is David Price, whose company, David Price Food Services, is based in Wallsend near Newcastle.

34 *A Shannon artic at Bridgwater.*

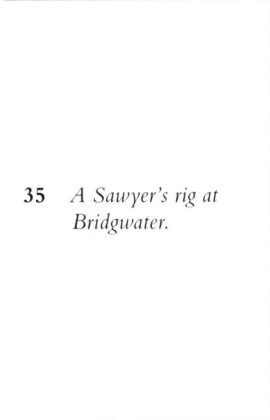

35 *A Sawyer's rig at Bridgwater.*

36 *David Price trailer with Langdons tractor.*

Between 1975 and 1987 David ran a company supplying fish to the wholesale trade, selling it to a national haulier in 1985. He formed David Price Food Services in 1987 and, following a Compulsory Purchase Order, in 1991 built a temperature-controlled store at Wallsend which now holds 6,000 pallets. David extended his coverage of the north with the depot he opened near Doncaster in 2006, closing the ChillNet gap between Peterborough and Wallsend in the east and, in the west, between Knowsley and Glasgow. David Price Food Services now operates 40 vehicles from the two depots, all of which carry the ChillNet roundel.

The hub concept relies on the ability of each driver to do a round trip within his permitted hours. Where the hubs are too far apart for this, as between Wallsend and Bridgwater, the two drivers meet halfway and exchange trailers, which is why you will see a tractor in one partner's livery pulling a trailer in another's. The Bridgwater yard is seldom without its complement of STL, Sawyers and David Price trailers.

The least economical or most difficult of the ChillNet operations was that servicing the south-east corner of England. The distances from Luton to Kent or Sussex are not great but the journey through or round London is an immense obstacle, with traffic congestion making it impossible to predict accurately times for collection or delivery. Langdons had examined without success a number of proposals to deal with the problem, from setting up its own depot near Tilbury to finding another partner, but Rupert Ryall eventually suggested a solution.

As in most industries, the fact they work for different firms does not prevent managers being on good personal terms with their counterparts in rival companies. Rupert had met Will Rayson and Danny Pye when they were with the transport and distribution company, Rokold, and kept in touch with them when they joined Nagel UK in Dover. The Nagel Group, based in Germany, had bought a Dover business to give it a foothold in the British market and was operating a number of refrigerated rigids for delivery in Kent, Sussex and South London. Rupert set up reciprocal arrangements whereby Langdons did distant work for Nagel and Nagel did local distribution for ChillNet, thereby making Dover the 12th ChillNet hub as well as the gateway for Langdons into Europe. It was an arrangement which was to have a profound and beneficial outcome for both parties, as we will observe in due time. At this point we will content ourselves with noting that in 2006 Langdons took over from Nagel UK the management of the Dover depot, apart from its European forwarding function, including its fine new refrigerated store on the outskirts of the town.

The participation of companies under different ownership in the ChillNet operation is not an ideal arrangement. There is, for example, no mechanism for ensuring that each partner offers identical rates to customers for the same services, nor is it always easy to ensure that reciprocal traffic between two firms under different ownership is evenly balanced. A friendly and trusting relationship between individuals has hitherto ensured that any differences have been amicably resolved, but as the business grows, and all the participants grow with it, it may be more difficult to operate in this way.

37 *Map of ChillNet hubs.*

All the ChillNet partners depend on the skill and quality of the depot managers, whose responsibilities include not just traffic and warehouse operations, but the supervision of drivers and other staff. Piers Graham-Hill took over as Transport Manager at Bridgwater from Arran Osman. Margaret Butler and Colin Payne at Luton, and David Couzens at Knowsley, joined Langdons from Tom Granby. Tony Kane is depot manager at Peterborough, Jeremy Edwin at Redditch and Danny Pye at Dover. These are the people with whom Rob Swindells, Rupert Ryall and Chris Davies liaise on a daily basis, which brings us back to examining how Langdons handles the ChillNet marketing.

The sales team keeps pace with the ChillNet customer list, now numbering over 1,500, because each new user of the service through Langdons has to obtain a credit rating from Bridgwater before being activated on any other basis other than pre-payment. Like every other manager, Rob Swindells and his colleagues have access to all operational data, including the daily discrepancy reports, which may refer to anything from a damaged box on a pallet to a late delivery. The information for every customer's daily business gives the job number, the collection point, the delivery address, the number of pallets, the depots involved, the order number, the method by which the order was placed, the rate table used for charging, the job price, the invoicing date and the POD information. Some orders are sent by telephone or voice mail, subject to written confirmation, but the majority, including those from new customers, are placed through the internet using the Langdons' websites, which also give a wealth of well-arranged information, even catering for those who take pleasure in recording the details of the Langdons' vehicles they see, or truck-spotting.

Tariffs, and the division of territories between hubs, are dictated by postcodes. The publication of tariffs makes it easy for competitors to undercut prices on an individual account, or even to offer to charge less than Langdons for a particular job. That would be a concern if they were able to offer the same service and reliability, but this is seldom the case, and the customer who is attracted to a competitor by the hope of a cheaper deal usually returns to ChillNet after three or four months.

ChillNet is an attractive business in several respects. The volume does not depend on a number of large customers, any one of whom is liable from time to time to seek competitive quotations or move to another supplier. The profit margins on large accounts are usually low, with supermarkets being notorious for the pressure on and demands from their suppliers, and even insisting on their using a nominated haulier who may charge the supplier a rate negotiated by the supermarket above what is available on the open market. (How much the supermarket charges the nominated haulier for negotiating the deal is a matter for conjecture.) Having numerous smaller credit accounts also reduces the risk of incurring a large bad debt. Food is the last commodity to be affected in an economic downturn, which means that the demand for temperature-controlled services is constant. Despite being much more complex than retail work (the delivery of a full load to a single destination), the shared-user system offers greater stability and a higher margin. Although Langdons is not looking for expansion in retail, it continues to accept business on an *ad hoc* basis in addition to its long-term relationship with Gerber Juices and its work for Nagel Group companies based in Europe.

Rob Swindells is responsible for ChillNet publicity material, including leaflets, the occasional stand at a trade show, the websites and advertisements in trade papers. The partners in the consortium share the cost of this publicity in proportion to the number of depots they operate. Thus Langdons, with six depots, pays half, STL and David Price pay a sixth each, and DHL/Exel and Sawyers pay one twelfth. The participants discuss and agree about publicity, along with tariffs and other matters of mutual interest or concern, at their regular policy meetings.

The department where Rob Swindells and Rupert Ryall have actively to seek work on occasion is the sale of sub-zero pallet storage. When, in 2006, Gerber built its own temperature-controlled warehouse in Bridgwater, it enabled Langdons finally to quit and sell the site at Walford Cross, and allowed the conversion of a further part of its Bridgwater store from chilled to sub-zero. Apart from the weeks leading up to Christmas, when food manufacturers stockpile things such as desserts, chilled goods remain in store only for short periods while sub-zero storage may be indefinite. We will look next at the storage side of the business, which is as important, if less glamorous, than the transport. Meanwhile, let us digest some of the lessons we may have noted about sales and commercial matters.

- Do not become over-reliant on any large customer.
- Use the worldwide web as a marketing tool.
- Make tariffs freely available to customers.
- Remember that a satisfied customer is your best advertisement.
- Leave low margin business to your competitors.
- Turnover for its own sake is vanity.

Chapter 20

STORE-KEEPING, PICKING, AND LOADING

Until a disastrous fire at Wiveliscombe in 1969, Tone Vale Transport had been as much an ambient warehousing business as a haulage company. So long as it remained in ambient transport, its successor, Langdons, had accepted long-term storage of anything from beer cans to used car tyres, which took the place of the diminishing reels of paper for Varma and the fertilizers for ICI. Some of these goods involved onward delivery while others just stayed there until, as was the case with the tyres, the company had to pay to get rid of them. In 1994, you may recall, Langdons did not operate temperature-controlled stores, apart from the one at Arnos Castle occupied by Tom Granby and another which it leased as a general cold store in Whitby Road, Bristol. After the fortuitous exit from Arnos Castle, and the disposal of Whitby Road, the company had progressively converted its Walford Cross store into refrigerated units, first to accommodate the Gerber chilled juice business and then also for ChillNet.

The Gerber business provided a good education for Langdons' managers and staff because it involved holding stocks of various juices in different sizes with short shelf-life for several retailers. As orders arrived direct from Gerber's customers for delivery the next day, the boxes of juice had to be assembled on to pallets (known as 'picking') and the pallets stretch-wrapped to contain the individual boxes and then loaded for delivery. The store men need to know precisely where each item was located, keep meticulous records of broken batches (where boxes have been taken from a stored pallet to make up a load), and ensure that stock was rotated so that the sell-by dates were observed. As the orders arrive in the early afternoon for delivery the next day, co-ordination between the store and the traffic controller has to be faultless. Especially in the early days, when loading bays were at a premium, there was no time for trailers to linger on the ramp while an order was being picked.

Sometimes an order arrived from a Gerber customer which could not be fully satisfied because there was no, or insufficient, inventory of one or more of the items. Any delay waiting for shortages to be made good from the factory caused congestion. Part, or 'short', deliveries were equally troublesome, involving extra documentation and the risk that the whole might be rejected by the retailer when it arrived at its destination.

The staff were able to keep pace with the growth of ChillNet because the concept evolved slowly and they were being taught by the two experienced managers who joined Langdons when Tom Granby handed over the South West. ChillNet does not involve picking, but with shared-user collection and delivery it is essential to know at all times the location of every pallet, and be able to extract the one which is required without having to shift others. The accurate preparation of identification labels for each pallet is essential and was the first task assigned to Spencer Dixon when he took over the IT function. The next move will be the bar-coding of individual pallets, to link up with all the other documentation.

For optimum efficiency and store utilisation, you need different con-figuration of racking and marshalling space for the categories of business. With long-term storage and full-load delivery, the racking can be fixed, tall and deep, with high density in the store. As trailers may be loaded direct from the racking, the space inside the loading bays devoted to marshalling loads can be limited. Holding stock for picking and retail delivery demands more flexible racking so that the store men do not have to move too many other pallets to reach the one they require. There is also no need to surrender racking space in the store to facilitate the marshalling of loads.

An operation such as ChillNet only works if every pallet can be identified and reached without a search or delay. It is desirable to provide a space behind each loading bay as long as each trailer so that a full load can be marshalled and checked before loading commences. This eliminates error and allows a quick turn around for vehicles. It also permits the store men to load using fork-lift trucks driven into the trailer rather than pallet-carriers steered on foot. Although both rigids and artics are able to back up to the loading bay and obtain a cold-seal while the doors are open, the quicker the turn around, the less the temperature change and the greater the throughput. To facilitate collection and delivery from the premises of a customer where there are no loading bays, Langdons' rigids are fitted with tail-lifts.

Chris Murt, who had moved from Avonmouth to Walford Cross in 1985 and became Transport Manager in 1987, was keenly aware that he could not run an efficient fleet unless it were backed up by a first-class warehousing operation. He therefore combined his duties in the traffic office with supervising the stores. The early development of ChillNet depended for the most part on depots which were not then under Langdons' control. Not content with organising his own warehouse, Chris would leave Walford Cross from time to time to sort out their problems and train their staff. Being a perfectionist, he was reluctant to return to his traffic office until his standards had been achieved, and from time to time Michael Donoghue had to suggest that he was also needed closer to home. Chris was, however, correct in his priorities. The ChillNet operation has to be seamless, with not just warehouses and transport in the same depot working in harmony but also between the participants in the consortium.

There are few industries in which individuals are given so much unsuper-vised responsibility as in road transport. The driver of a rig costing £100,000

38   *Chilled racking at Bridgwater.*

may be carrying a load which is even more valuable, and for most of his working hours he is on his own. The store man works in a team, but also bears great responsibility. Errors in marshalling loads can cost thousands of pounds. Although provided with protective clothing, not everyone likes working in a chilled environment, while a temperature of minus 25°C is even less agreeable. An unexpected benefit is that those who work under these conditions seldom seem to catch the common cold.

Just as the drivers depend on competent traffic operators, so the store men need able supervisors. Chris Murt is fortunate to rely on colleagues such as John Baker, Scott Walker, the Fitzavon brothers, Justin Spires and Danny Pye. These managers are responsible for the recruitment and training of their staff. Safe working practices are a priority in an environment where loads are heavy and fork-lift trucks move swiftly. Staff have to ensure that the loads are correctly placed on the axles of trailers and that rigs are not overloaded. All Langdons' tractors are six-wheelers and have a maximum weight limit of 44 tonnes, but four-wheeled tractors, such as many arriving from continental Europe, have a limit of 38 tonnes and trailers must be more lightly laden.

As with all staff, honesty is a prime requirement in a store man. As the job can involve lifting, strength and fitness are important, as are time-keeping and

39 *The Knowsley depot, Liverpool.*

regular attendance. Even where packaging has been damaged or a sell-by date has expired, and Langdons have been told to dispose of the goods, employees are not permitted to remove anything from a store. If staff were allowed to take away items which had become undeliverable, the temptation to put a tine of a fork-lift truck through a box might prove irresistible. For a time, hating to throw away good stock, Chris Murt tried to operate a system under which he issued chits permitting employees to take goods which would otherwise end up in a disposal skip. It was not a success. It proved impossible to check what had been loaded on to outgoing vehicles over and above what appeared on the manifest, just as it was difficult to judge whether damage to a shroud-wrapped pallet in the store was deliberate or accidental.

Langdons operates the stores in only four of its six depots, the other two at Luton and Peterborough being managed by TDG. In November 2006 Gerber moved its inventory to a new store of its own at Express Park in Bridgwater, leaving its operation to experienced Langdons' staff. This made more space available in the company's own depot, especially for sub-zero storage. Gerber remained Langdons' largest retail customer but, with so many competitors in the retail delivery business, the margins remained lower than for the more difficult shared-user work. The volumes were also less predictable, with supermarkets liable to change suppliers or insist on the use of a nominated haulier, in which case Langdons does the difficult work of picking the load while a competitor gets the simple job of transporting it. Another problem with retail work is that it may be difficult to find a return load after delivery to an RDC, although the timing of some RDC deliveries means that the vehicle can be double-shifted, doing local work by day.

Looking to the future, it would seem that Langdons will concentrate to an increasing extent on the most difficult sector of the industry, shared-user, single or more pallet, temperature-controlled, rapid delivery, fixed-price work. It is also helpful to be able to offer the smaller producers short-term refrigerated storage space so that they can produce in greater volume than is required for daily delivery and pay less for collection by assembling larger loads. Some 80 per cent of food and drink product from larger manufacturers is delivered to retail, but there remains a significant volume of other traffic. In any business, the simpler the operation, the greater the competition and the lower the margins. Conversely, the more complex the operation, the fewer the competitors and the higher the margins. As any clever student knows, it is easier to excel if the examination paper is difficult.

These days Chris Murt's skills are widely recognised and he is sometimes asked to accompany Rupert Ryall on Customer Service visits. Although he is responsible for some 10,000 pallet spaces, with thousands of cross-docking and loading movements a day, his insistence on safety is such that his stores have never had a pallet-related accident. When he claims that Langdons has established in ChillNet 'the Recorded Delivery of the chilled and frozen

40   *The Dover depot.*

pallet world', he is doing no more than stating the magnitude of his and his colleagues' achievements and recognising the importance of ChillNet to small food producers up and down the land.

> The use of 'store men' rather than 'store people' is not just a literary convention. As with policing, the job requires physical attributes as well as skill. Society may be obliged to tolerate urban disorder and no-go areas as a by-product of deference to equal opportunities in the public sector. In the private sector, fitness to do the job has to be the prime consideration.

- Ensure close co-operation between transport and warehouse.
- Do not allow any staff to remove items from the warehouse even if they cannot be delivered and have to be destroyed.
- Have facilities to store buffer stocks for small producers.
- Use a rigorous system of pallet identification.
- Offer customers a seamless service.
- Provide adequate marshalling areas behind loading bays.

Chapter 21

THE NAGEL GROUP ACQUIRES LANGDONS

W hen Michael Donoghue became Chairman of Langdons in 2000, he continued to combine that office with his position as Chief Executive. During the many years that I was working with him, an important part of my role had been to suggest that he think again about some of the proposals which continually emerged from his fertile brain. The majority of them might, on reflection, appear impracticable or untimely, and the trick was to encourage those that, however unconventional, would benefit the business, of which the establishment of the truck stop at Walford Cross was an example. After I had left, Michael retained the services of William Underwood and John Rix, who were non-executive, but saw the advantage of appointing another director who would be familiar with the day-to-day running of the business, as I had been, yet sufficiently detached and experienced to act as his sounding board and curb his enthusiasms.

You may recall that Rob Holder, a Chartered Accountant and member of WMAS, had taken the nominal position of Finance Director of Langdons at the time of the MBO in 1986. He remained on the board but his private client practice and other business interests made it impossible for him to do more than act in an advisory position. Langdons tried on two subsequent occasions to recruit a Finance Director from outside the firm, but didn't find a suitably qualified person who fitted in with the conscientious but relaxed way in which it operated. When the post became vacant again in 1999, Simon Holder, another member of WMAS, was drafted in on a part-time basis. When Michael Donoghue became Chairman, Simon proved adept at counselling him, advising on commercial matters, helping Sheila Burnett in personnel management and liaising on accounts issues with David Every-Clayton and his team.

Simon had qualified as a Chartered Accountant at the age of 21 but had not practised professionally, his entire career being spent within industry. At the age of 28 he had become, with two others, the owner of an engineering company. When one of his partners reneged on an agreement to retire at the age of 65, Simon sold his shares, left the company, and began working part-time for other manufacturing firms in which he had invested, mainly in and around Bristol. There is no industrial discipline as strict as that taught by your

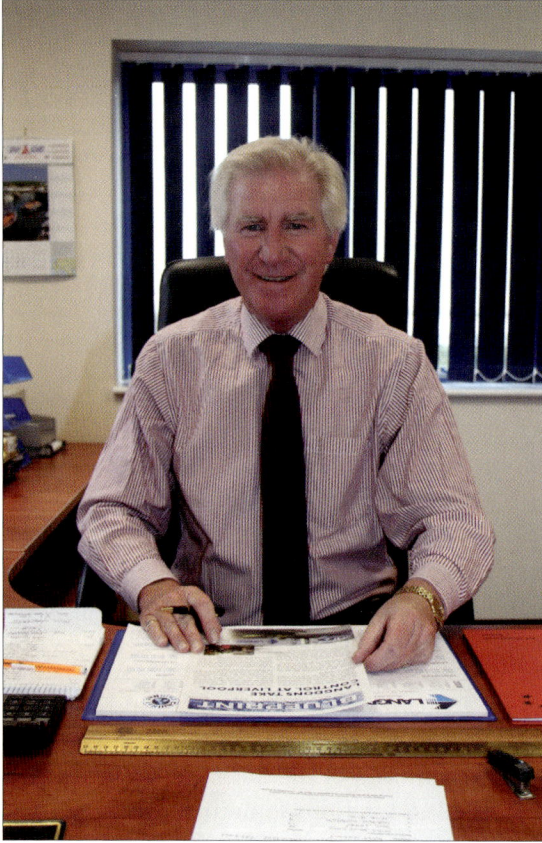

41 *Michael Donoghue.*

using your own cash in your own business. If the business fails, you may lose your job and go bankrupt. (If you are an employee only, and the business fails, you may lose your job. If you work in the public sector, however dismal the performance, you keep your job and the business will never fail.) Simon had therefore the right mindset needed to work beside Michael Donoghue, Paul Rowe and Rob Swindells, all of whom had had to risk incurring personal debt when they bought Langdons in 1986. As part owner of WMAS, he was also indirectly a substantial shareholder in Langdons.

After 27 years managing the company and with 'time's winged chariot hurrying near', Michael Donoghue, Paul Rowe and Rob Swindells recognised in good time the need to identify and train their successors. By 2000, in every department, younger men and women were already accepting greater responsibility. With few exceptions, recruitment from outside the company had been less successful than guidance and promotion from within. It was gratifying to see that the younger directors on the board in 2007, Arran Osman, Patrick Griffiths, Spencer Dixon and Rupert Ryall, had all, as it were, come through the ranks. After resolving the dilemma of finding their successors in management, and having discovered in Simon Holder the right Financial Director, the MBO team faced a more difficult issue. They needed to find a way of passing on the ownership of Langdons to a sympathetic buyer or to investors who would not break up the company.

The preferred option would have been a sale to the next generation of managers and other staff. Unfortunately the net assets of the business alone, without any allowance for goodwill, revaluation of freehold property, or other considerations, amounted to some £8 million. Any venture capitalist willing to finance another MBO would almost certainly seek an exit within three or four years, just as those who had supported the Taunton Cider management had made it a condition of their involvement that the shares should be publicly quoted, enabling the venture capitalists to take their profit and move on.

Another option was to sell to a larger competitor. There had, over the years, been no shortage of companies within the industry which had approached the board offering to buy Langdons. A motley assortment of brokers, carpetbaggers and opportunists had also offered their services to put a deal together. Michael

42 *Simon Holder.*

Donoghue and his colleagues knew that any larger national company which bought Langdons would probably want to use it only as a depot based in the West Country, with many administrative functions being performed elsewhere. Drivers and store men would keep their jobs, along with immediate support staff, but many of the loyal people who had helped to create such a successful business might be made redundant.

The introduction in 1997 of outside investors, who had bought 28 per cent of the company to finance the building of a new warehouse for Sunny Delight, might have offered another way to transfer ownership without risk if an unofficial market in the shares had evolved through the local firm of stock brokers, some of whose clients had invested. A gradual increase in the number of outside investors, with the board retaining the right to refuse to register a transfer to a party of which it disapproved, could have afforded security to all the staff and allowed the majority shareholders gradually to reduce their investment. In the event, during the seven years after 1997, none of the new investors had wanted to sell any shares, nor was there any pressure from them to change the status quo. What had seemed a possible exit strategy for the original MBO team had not proved feasible in practice.

It would have been possible, albeit expensive, in 2002 to have floated the shares to one of the junior stock markets. The introduction would have been unusual because the company did not need to raise fresh capital. Here again, the spectre of Taunton Cider's fate, and the loss of hundreds of jobs, loomed. If Langdons became a quoted company, it would not be long, the directors feared, before one of the unsuccessful suitors within the industry made a bid which the majority of new shareholders would accept.

At that juncture, Will Rayson, who was working for Nagel UK in Dover, told Rupert Ryall that the Nagel Group was looking to buy another transport company in the United Kingdom. It had proved difficult for the management of the Dover depot to handle both the domestic market within the United Kingdom and the cross-Channel traffic. Because the Nagel Group was based in Germany, any business which it acquired in Britain larger than that at Dover would remain the dominant partner within the United Kingdom, and there would be no local Head Office to take over the functions performed by the existing Langdons' staff. A tie with the Nagel Group also offered the prospect of increased opportunities for ChillNet and other business into and out of Europe.

Michael Schymik, the far-sighted German manager at Dover, was enthusiastic about the Nagel Group buying Langdons and initiated discussions with Simon Holder which led to their recommending such a deal to the Nagel Group and to the board of Langdons. None of Langdons' directors or shareholders was against a plan which safeguarded all jobs and offered stability for the future, even though the price would almost certainly be considerably lower than what might have been achieved by selling to the highest bidder or floating the company on the stock market. The negotiations were protracted, not least by the 'law's delays', but eventually the parties agreed terms and the deal was consummated with effect from 26 October 2004. John Rix and William Underwood then left the board, and Michael Schymik joined it.

A business is normally valued after considering its assets, its profit record and its potential. In 2004 a privately owned company might expect to have been assessed as worth between seven and ten times its annual profit before tax. Langdons was unusual in that its assets had traditionally been undervalued in its balance sheet with, for example, trailers being written down to £100 after hire-purchase payments ceased even though they still had years of future use. The reserves included as liabilities on the balance sheet were, to say the least, conservative. (The only time I was asked as Chairman formally to meet our Inspector of Taxes was to discuss whether or not our reserves at the year end were excessive.) Despite contemplating a sale, the directors made no effort to increase short-term profitability by, for example, delaying investment which would only pay off over the longer term, and a lower profit of £260,855 was reported in 2004 because of a significant spend on ChillNet development, including the heavy start-up costs and initial loss at Redditch. Pricing the business on a multiple of its current profit would produce a figure much below its true worth, while the full potential of ChillNet was still conjectural.

The directors knew that, just as the profit had been conservatively reported, the declared assets were also undervalued. They believed that, in ChillNet, the company had developed a business with great potential, although no goodwill figure or carrying forward of start-up costs had been credited in the balance sheet. They decided, however, that it was better to recommend to shareholders acceptance of an offer based on the declared asset value of the company which came from a buyer who would leave the firm as it was, rather than seek a higher price from a purchaser who would not guarantee continuity of Langdons as an independent business with security of employment for all who worked there.

Kurt Nagel, who owned the Nagel Group, was equally realistic, appreciating the importance of retaining the management and structure of Langdons. He was anxious that the four original MBO partners – Michael Donoghue, Paul Rowe, Rob Swindells and WMAS – should not just remain with the business but be financially interested in its future, for at least five years. On completion of the sale, the 'outside' shareholders received payment in full at a price which reflected the increase in the value of the company during their seven-year tenure. The employees who held share options, other than the directors who renounced their own rights, were also satisfied in full. The four original partners agreed to be paid for their shares over the five years of their continuing employment, thereby demonstrating their confidence in the future of Langdons as part of the Nagel Group. The growth in the company's turnover and profit in the following three years was equally gratifying to all those involved. The turnover rose to £50 million a year while the profit before tax for the three years amounted to £4.8 million, of which half was due to exceptional items following the settlement of the loan by Procter and Gamble and the sale of the freehold of Walford Cross.

43 *Kurt Nagel.*

The Nagel Group was the ideal owner for a firm with the ethos of Langdons. Kurt Nagel's father had started it in 1935 with one 10-ton tractor and trailer to service the meat and sausage industry in the region of Versmold, which is situated in the area lying between Bielefeld, Münster and Osnabrück. As with Langdons, he lost his vehicles to the military during the war but was subsequently able to re-establish his business in temperature-controlled distribution. His son, also called Kurt, joined him in 1982 and became proprietor when his father died in 1992. Sadly, Kurt Nagel junior died in February 2008 at the age of 46, leaving his family with a business which operated 4,000 refrigerated vehicles from 65 depots in 15 countries, and employed 6,500 people.

Apart from the advantages of tying up with the leading temperature-controlled operator on the continent of Europe (despite the tragic death of Kurt Nagel), Langdons benefits from working with people who share the same business philosophy and approach to customers and to staff. The Nagel Group, like Langdons, has prospered because it offers producers throughout Europe the best service for the warehousing, picking and delivery of chilled or sub-zero produce at published rates. Within the Nagel Group, help is available from the centre for those needing assistance, but, as Langdons has discovered, there is minimal interference in the management of an efficient subsidiary. The Group, like Langdons, pays close attention to the training of employees because it, too, believes that every individual is important. And the managers in Germany are wise enough to leave well alone.

Only one of the many Nagel subsidiaries is at present involved primarily in ambient distribution. Having for its customers manufacturers whose products include ambient as well as temperature-controlled foods, the demand for a comprehensive service may in due course affect Langdons as well as the Nagel Group. There may also be an opportunity to make available for small producers in the many other countries in which the Nagel Group operates the ChillNet formula which has proved so successful in the United Kingdom and Ireland.

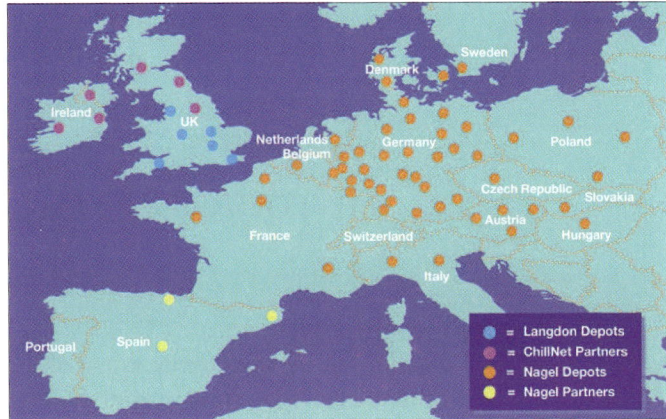

44 *Map of Europe with Nagel depots.*

Whatever the future holds, it appears that in accepting the offer from Kurt Nagel the shareholders in Langdons may have foregone a higher price for their shares but they have achieved a secure future for those who have helped them turn the company into the most efficient operator of temperature-controlled transport and distribution services within the United Kingdom.

- Plan for succession both in management and ownership.
- The highest bid may not be the wisest choice.
- Never forget those who have loyally served your company.
- If it ain't broke, don't fix it.
- *Viel Geld heißt nicht immer viel Glück.*

Chapter 22

AUTHOR'S NOTE

A transport and distribution network is the essential link between production and consumption. If it were to cease operating, within a week society would collapse. Manufacturers and producers function only to the extent that their goods can be delivered to distant customers with whom they have no personal contact. Consumers survive because goods and produce from afar are available at all times in local outlets. The service works so well that people seldom give it a thought.

More than a million people are employed in the transport and distribution industry within the United Kingdom. Like the Victorian civil and mechanical engineers who wrought the industrial revolution, few of them are graduates. Their discipline is not usually taught in universities nor is it a subject which commonly attracts academic research or publication. Their achievement in improving productivity by fifty times in as many years goes unnoticed, but their achievement benefits everyone.

It is important for society not just that the industry continues to perform well but that it does so causing the minimum congestion and pollution. The more efficient the organisation, the better the loading factor, the fewer the vehicles on the road.

A study of the Langdons operation may be of interest to those in business in two respects. The management style, financial control, use of IT, and respect for the individual employee follow a pattern which is normal in successful organisations and should be emulated by all. In particular, other firms engaged in distribution may benefit from comparing Langdons' operational procedures with their own.

Managers in the public sector could also learn how to use their resources more effectively by studying the bullet points. Those who work in a successful organisation, offering a reliable and prompt service, enjoy their jobs more than those where the service is poor and grudging. Over-manning and the retention of incompetent staff are demoralising for all. Where there is no sanction for failure, it may be less stressful for managers in the short term to live with rather than tackle inefficiency but, as I know from personal experience, those who grasp the nettle are amply rewarded in the longer term by the improvement in the performance of the organisation, the morale of those who work there, and the gratitude of those who depend upon it.

The obstacles Langdons faced in trying to expand in the district of Taunton Deane, which led to the firm's relocation elsewhere, are not exceptional. (Two manufacturing companies for which I worked in Taunton were similarly frustrated: in one case it took two appeals to obtain planning permission to build a second factory and in the other we were rescued by the Crown Estate, which can develop without planning permission. Both companies are now, like Langdons, in foreign ownership.) If a local authority wishes to benefit from hosting a mixed economy and low unemployment, it should understand the imperatives under which industry operates. It is wiser to foster the business it has than to try to attract an outsider. Nor should officials seek to justify their existence by exhibiting 'the insolence of office' or through initiating criminal proceedings against a reputable firm in respect of a trivial technical offence.

Politicians also have lessons to learn. Taxing British road transport more heavily than any of its peers in other industrialised countries puts up the cost of living for everyone and gives an unfair advantage to foreign hauliers visiting the United Kingdom. With rail entrepôt depots derelict, talk of taking goods traffic off the roads is fanciful. Laws which allow privileged categories of employee not to report for work when they choose, and make it difficult for an employer to dismiss them if they are incompetent, are counter-productive. In the private sector, firms cannot afford to carry passengers nor is it good for the economy or society to try to compel them to do so. To protect themselves, they will be increasingly reluctant to offer work to privileged applicants, with unfortunate social consequences.

My thanks are due to Rob Swindells, who asked me to write this book, and for the Nagel Group who have supported the publication. I also take this opportunity to acknowledge my debt to my many friends within Langdons who have helped me with technical detail and still kindly treat me as a member of the family.

R.W. Holder
West Monkton

Glossary

artic	an articulated vehicle
BDC	the Bristol Development Corporation
BRS	British Road Services, the nationalised road haulage operation
cross-docking	taking goods into or out of a store and especially the unloading from one vehicle to load directly on to another
curtain-sider	a trailer covered with waterproof sheets of material on a framework; also known by the trade name Tautliner
DBC	the Danish Bacon Company
EGR	exhaust gas recycling
flat bed	a trailer without sides
IBC	intermediate bulk container, a large square floppy bag used industrially for carrying powders
IT	information technology
LGV	Large Goods Vehicle as defined by law
MBO	a Management Buy-out of a company from its corporate owner
picking	taking elements from various sources to assemble on a single pallet
POD	proof of delivery – a form acknowledging receipt of a load
prime mover	a commercial road vehicle with a motor
RDC	a Regional Distribution Centre of a supermarket chain
retail	selling directly to the public in volume and taking full loads
rigid	a vehicle in which the load carrying department is integral with the chassis and engine
selling wheels	carrying a full load between two fixed points
SCR	selective catalytic reduction
shared user	conveying deliveries for different customers on the same vehicle
sheeting	placing and roping down a waterproof cover over a load on a flat-bed trailer
shrouding	using material to surround the sides and top of a pallet
shunter	an unlicensed articulated tractor used for moving trailers in a yard
stretch wrapping	containing a load on a pallet with material round the sides
subbie	a sub-contractor working for others on an *ad hoc* basis
tachograph	a device for recording all movements of a vehicle
TDG	The Transport Development Group
tipping	discharging a load
TKM	Tozer, Kemsley and Millbourn, the conglomerate which sold Langdons to the management
tractor	a vehicle with a cab used to pull a detachable trailer
trunking	taking a load from one hub or depot to another
wiring	illegally tampering with a tachograph to stop it recording
WMAS	West Monkton Advisory Services Ltd, a company established by the Holder family to advise and to invest in businesses which were in financial difficulty or subject to Management Buy-outs

INDEX